An Unlit Path

One Family's Journey Toward the Light of Truth

Deborah L. Hannah

This book is dedicated to
all the families
who have come before us
and all
who will come after,
each willing to walk
an unlit path;

To all those
who are willing to
risk everything
for the sake of a child;

And finally to those
who have found,
and to those
who are still searching for,
the incredible healing power
of forgiveness.

Contents

*"However,
if you suffer
as a Christian,
do not
be ashamed,
but praise
God
that you bear
that name."*

1 Peter 4:16

Introduction

Reflections on a Life Once Lived

"Give yourself fully to God.
He will use you to accomplish great things on the
condition that you believe much more in His love
than in your own weakness."
Mother Theresa

Today I found the courage to open my front door, looking out as if for the first time. I saw to the west, the mountains of Colorado, and to the east, the sun rising in an array of colors. I am sure this happens every day; today, however, was the first time in over two years that I had allowed myself to see it. As I stepped out, the crisp spring air swept gently across my face, creating a stark contrast to the long lonely winter I had now survived. The truth is it was not just a winter; I had somberly watched as each season took its turn. Once so aware of the magnificence of nature, now I could not even fathom how much I had missed. I longed to leave my safe haven and rejoin the world, but I was haunted by visions of a past I could not escape.

As I walked out on the veranda I remembered it as a beautiful place, once used for the gathering of family and friends and the sharing of stories and laughter; now at its best it was merely an anxiety-provoking extension of my personal refuge. Leaves, debris and other evidence of abandonment cluttered the flooring; tumbleweeds overshadowed traces of large blooming rose bushes, and the deafening sound of silence drowned out the sounds of a life once lived. The sentence of my self-imposed imprisonment had ended, and freedom was mine, if only I could find the courage to accept it.

Each sight, each sound, each smell reminded me of what I so wanted to forget. I had many reasons for not coming out here anymore, and it was not only who or what I would see, but also who would see me. I wished foremost for anonymity. I had been here only a moment, and already I missed the safety of my sanctuary. Still, I had to stay, because this day could not be one of fear; it could only be one of truth. The leaves left lying where they had fallen months before crackled with the wind; suddenly my mind drifted to five years earlier.

I remembered walking out of the front door of Fort Lewis, the state mental hospital, when then too I noticed the leaves; they were falling in the night breeze. It was cold, and I was frightened. I looked back as I heard the hollow metal clang of the door shutting behind me. I pulled my collar up around my neck to protect myself from the night air, I suppose, or perhaps instead from whatever demons I sensed I needed protection.

I heard emanating from within the walls the disturbing sounds of people distressed by something they did not understand. I then felt the presence of someone's eyes watching me as if he were aware of how truly frightened I was. I reached for my keys; I wanted them in my hands when I found my car. I did not want to take even one extra moment at a place where I did not belong. I wondered if the man who was watching me thought he belonged there, or if he too shared my denial.

I looked toward my car and the distance I would need to walk. The man, once hidden, now stood openly on the side of the building. I debated in my mind if I should wait in the safety of the light, accepting those demons that waited therein, or if I should venture out, because despite the danger it was at least an attempt to reclaim my sanity.

I began walking briskly; to my dismay, he followed. I walked faster and faster; each step I took I felt him behind me. I had begun to run by the time I reached my car; I fumbled with the key to get it in the lock, sure that at any moment he would reach out and grab me. The door unlocked, I pulled it open and quickly I was in; and just as quickly, I locked the door again. I looked around, but to my disbelief, I could not see him anywhere. I sat in the dark, weeping and wondering what was real and what was not.

Had a man really been there at all? Maybe it was what he represented that frightened me. Was I afraid that if I did not leave this place what he had I would have also? Was I afraid I already did and he sensed it? Did he know of the last few years of my life and the depth of the darkness I had been drawn into? Did he know I belonged there, probably more than he? I do not know who he was or what he represented; all I knew for sure was that I had to leave this place and I never wanted to come back.

I looked around me. I had left that place, and five years had since passed. I was home, but the home I once knew no longer existed. My memories, once so real, were now only witnesses to an illusion. Feeling weak, I looked at the old rocking chair swaying in the wind; it called out to me with the squeak of an eerie rhythm. I remembered singing to children as they sat in my lap on this chair, now empty and weathered by the years; it offered no proof of this past. Still, I sat down and began to rock. I wondered where the years had gone. I remembered happiness and true joy; yet now they were only a distant memory. I reached out to touch the crumpled brown rose that still clung to the vine. I watched it turn to ash in my fingers; but to my amazement it began to slowly regain its beautiful red color. Not so, for the red was simply an indication of the thorn piercing my skin. I thought of how often I had made that same mistake, confusing betrayal for beauty.

I was brought back to a day only two years prior, when then too I felt the thorn of deceit. It was the afternoon I learned where my children were; they had been missing for what seemed an eternity. The nightmare of not knowing what had happened to them was over; only now a new nightmare had begun, accepting the betrayal hidden in that truth.

No one would speak *to* me, instead only *about* me; the truth was now lies, and lies now the truth. The betrayal continued as I learned the people I once counted as dear friends and confidants had known all along where my children were and decided not to tell me. What I once saw as beautiful, my family and my friends, was now only the piercing thorn.

I wiped the blood from my hand; if only the blood of their betrayal could have so easily been washed away. I rocked a little longer trying to remember why it was that I had not wanted to come out here for so long. I remembered such happy times, but those thoughts were sharply interrupted by the memory of a loud knock on the front door.

I had answered it with no fear or trepidation; I had not known such emotions yet. It was the police, followed by Social Services; they would teach me to experience those emotions each time thereafter. I lived in fear from that day to this, unable to regain the confidence and innocence that had marked my character prior to that knock. It was a defining moment in the life I had created; it was a defining moment in that life now lost. I remembered why I did not come out these doors for so long; for these were memories I wished had also been lost.

I found myself wiping the tears from my face. It was so painful to look back, so frightening to look forward, so lonely to stay present. I looked out toward the pond and saw a couple walking along. My first thought was to jump up and go back into my fortress. Instead, I put my head down and waited until they had passed. I had averted this threat, but I awaited the next apprehensively. I was beginning to understand it was not these walls that kept me captive; it was my own fear and self-doubt.

This doubt was birthed on a winter evening at the sheriff's department; my whole family was interrogated, each in our own rooms, and forced to write statements as to what had transpired over the past years. Once born, the doubt gave place to shame and guilt, which grew into a barbed wire fence around my heart, completing the imprisonment.

I could no longer sit in this rocking chair; these agonizing visions of the past were now becoming too painful to bear. I stood up as if trying to get away from them. But I knew the more difficult ones were yet to come. The memories of the hurtful times of deceit, betrayal and abandonment ripped out my heart. The memories of the times of love and trust and genuine joy left my heart intact to feel the depth of the wound over and over again.

Suddenly I heard the sound of a dog barking. I looked toward it and caught sight of the big blue van sitting in front of our house, as if telling the whole world who we were. This fifteen-passenger van had been our second home. We took it to baseball practice each day and to basketball games and wrestling tournaments. We took it on family outings, bowling and to the movies. We shared songs, laughter and always our love for one another in this van. Whether we were eating an ice cream cone in it or having a serious discussion about life, it was real.

People jokingly referred to it as "The Brady Bunch Van." We knew the Brady Bunch had nothing on us. The kids named it John Henry when they were young because it was so big and strong. We took it on vacations, and, yes, several of the children had even taken their turn getting sick in it. It was once full of a time in our lives when we knew happiness. Now it sat empty, the seats removed on the inside and rust beginning to take its toll on the outside. Like our lives, it too showed the wear and tear of the days gone by.

I wanted it gone, just as I had wanted to move from this home. I wanted to break free from the sights and sounds of who we once were and again claim the obscurity that now evaded us. Yet the van remained, perhaps because of our unwillingness to let go and perhaps because it was the validation of our truth. I walked toward it and, placing my hand on the side, sighed; I could almost hear the sounds of the children coming from within it. In reality, I knew it was nothing more than a beat-up old van, and no matter how much I wanted it to, it held no truth.

I walked back up to the porch with the nervous energy that is found when you walk but have no idea where you are going. I was on the porch again, safer than in the world, but not as safe as if I just went back in the house and decided to do this another day. Nevertheless, I had said that so many times before; this truly was another day. I had to wonder though; did reliving all this hurt serve any possible good? I needed to understand my life and its purpose. I knew of no other way to get it, so I continued.

I looked to the sign that hung above our front door. "Bienvenidos, mi casa es su casa," it read. We had brought that sign home with us from a cruise we had taken to Mexico, Joe and I and all the children. We loved traveling together, spending so much time learning of other cultures and other people. We had gone swimming in the ocean and horseback riding in the mountains. That trip was not a lie, was it? The hugs, the laughter, the intimacy of spirit had been real to me, but had they been real? In all this time I had not found the answer to that question; maybe I had been afraid to seek it. The only truth I knew was that I longed for those days and yet hated every memory of them.

As I walked back toward the rocking chair, I saw in the bushes, underneath a pile of withered leaves, an old worn football. I picked it up and in a futile effort tried to wipe the dirt off as if to bring it back to life. It reminded me of every Saturday afternoon in the fall. We would have several games to attend Joe, as football coach, and I, as cheerleading coach. We worked hard all week with each of the children to prepare for Saturdays. As I tossed the ball up and down in the air, I could almost hear the whistle of the referee, the sound of helmets hitting helmets and the echo of the girls cheering for their brothers. None of which was as loud as the scream of the crowd and the sound of parents trying to relive their youth. Those truly were the glory days, the days we were sure our children would never forget and the days we as parents would cherish.

I laid the ball down and again sat back in the rocking chair. This time it was harder than I remembered, offering no comfort to my growing uneasiness. There was no escape from the harshness of my reality. The harshness I felt; the reality I still could not sense. Is the truth the truth when only you believe it? Is an illusion an illusion if you cannot see through it? If I could find a way to perceive my reality, maybe I could accept it. To do that meant I would need to pick through the pieces, and instead of judging my life by brief visions and memories, I needed to look at the totality of what I had tried to do. Did the tragic consequences negate the premise, or was this in some way the predictable end to such a journey?

I took a sip of my tea, wrapped the afghan around my shoulders and settled in for the long process of remembering a past that most would choose to forget or at least admit no involvement in or liability to.

Chapter One

A Simple Knock

~~~~~~

Mark 9:37
"Whoever welcomes one of these little children
in my name welcomes me;
and whoever welcomes me
does not welcome me
but the one who sent me."

~~~~~~

My first thought in this long journey became how incredible it was that a simple knock on a door could forever change so many lives. It was never meant to. It was just a door; it was just a knock yet nothing would ever again be the same.

We had anticipated this moment, struggled over it and prayed about it. But, as with any knock on any door, there really is no way to know what lies behind it. Sometimes, it is possible to prepare or to have some expectation; in this case, we did not. We had our dreams, our hopes, our visions, but what we did not have was the knowledge to understand the likelihood of accomplishing those things.

We were the ones who had made the decision to bring a child into our home; we had made the phone call to Social Services and scheduled our orientation and training with Louis who would become our case manager. We were, however, surprised when the whole process took only several hours, a home visit and our physicals, and there we were foster parents. We chose it, but I must admit we felt ill prepared for what lay ahead. Our first mistake was in trusting that Social Services, or anyone else for that matter, were.

The county encouraged us. Joe, my husband, had been a foster child, and it had been a positive experience. He had always promised himself he would "pay it forward" to another young boy. In fact, one of his favorite poems read:

The Bridge Builder

An old man going a lone highway
Came to the evening, cold and gray,
To a chasm vast and wide and steep,
With waters rolling cold and deep.
The old man crossed in the twilight dim,
The sullen stream had no fear for him;
But he turned when safe on the other side,
And built a bridge to span the tide.

"Old man," said a fellow pilgrim near,
"You are wasting your strength with building here.

Your journey will end with the ending day,
You never again will pass this way.
You've crossed the chasm, deep and wide,
Why build you this bridge at eventide?"

The builder lifted his old gray head.
"Good friend, in the path I have come," he said,

"There followed after me today
A youth whose feet must pass this way.
The chasm that was at naught to me.
To that fair-haired youth may a pitfall be;
He too, must cross in the twilight dim-
Good friend, I am building this bridge for him."

-Will Allen Dromgoole

Yes, we were optimistic, but then again Joe had also been prophesized over years earlier and was told his life would involve many children and an inconceivable amount of pain. Was it possible the prophet was right and not Joe's own experience or even that of Social Services? We never took the time to examine that; we trusted in faith that this was what we had been led to do. We were young, hopeful, and ready to do our part to change the world.

There we were, all six of us, Joe and I and our four children, Mandy, Joey, Amy and Paul, huddled together on this tiny porch, preparing for that knock. At the family meeting we had agreed this was the right thing to do. We had prayed in the car on the way over, and now it was time. Yet we stood there, taking an extra moment before that knock. When it was done, the knock complete, we entered a world we would never be able to find our way back from, never be able to understand. We were in their world now, and we would never be able to change that world as much as it would change us.

The door opened so quickly it almost knocked us over. A woman suddenly appeared before us. She was average, middle-age, not attractive, not unattractive, just a woman. She looked at us and opened the door wider, allowing us to pass.

"So you here to see the kids?" she questioned.

"Yes, we were told by our caseworker, Louis, that a young boy in the age range we are looking for is staying here and needs a home."

"Yea, he does, but so does his older sister and his younger brother. They all need a home," she said sarcastically.

"Oh, I know," I answered, my voice now cracking. "Louis mentioned that, but we are looking for only one child. There would be no way for us to take three. I mean, look we already have four children. That would just be impossible."

I was not sure why I was spending so much time defending our decision. I guess I felt guilty we were not doing more.

"Right, right," she said as if she had heard it before. "Anyways, the kids are in the backyard. Go on out."

We began walking through the family room toward the backyard. Before we could get there, however, a beautiful, cherub-faced, blond-haired girl greeted us. She ran right up to us, no fear or hesitation, just the excitement of a child. She grabbed hold of my leg, and her blue eyes looked deeply into mine. Her hair hung in long curly locks.

The first words she ever spoke to me were, "Are you going to be my new mommy?" She had me right then, and she knew it.

"What is your name?" I asked.

"Marissa," she quipped. "What is yours?"

"My name is Debbie."

"Oh," she said. "I think I will still call you mom."

"How old are you?"

"I am eight. How old are you?"

We were then interrupted by the entrance into the room of one of the cutest kids I had ever seen. Like his sister, he had big blue eyes and blond hair. Both of the children looked so much alike; his name was Colton, and he was seven. Colton had on old tennis shoes that were ripped in the front so they would pop open as he walked. He had one loose tooth hanging in the front. I am not sure how it hung on, but Colton was not about to let anyone touch it. Quickly he turned to Joey and excitedly said, "Come on. Let's go play." They both headed off to the backyard.

I had not seen the little one yet, so I walked outside. He was sitting off to himself on the bench. He looked nothing like the other two. I knew him to have a different father; Colton and Marissa shared the same dad. Unlike them, this little one was shy and somewhat withdrawn. I tried to begin a conversation with him. He seemed to understand me, but I could not, if my life depended on it, make sense of one word he said. What he did say, he said with passion and would even occasionally laugh. I would laugh too, but I was only laughing at his incredible joy, not because I understood. I knew him to be four years old, and I knew his name to be William. I called him Willy; he seemed to like that.

Joe and I stepped back and watched the kids interact for a few minutes. They genuinely seemed to enjoy each other. We walked back inside to talk to the foster parents and find out more.

"They are good kids. We have had no real behavior problems. They struggle with rules a bit because they seem to have had open rein prior to coming here," the foster mom, Linda, said.

"What happened to their parents?" Joe asked.

"They were picked up in a drug raid about two months ago; the police broke into their room at the motel. They could not locate their mom or dad at that time but noted there was absolutely no food available for the children. Colton told them he was hungry because none of them had eaten in days. The police took them into custody only to find out there had been a long history of neglect. Social Services had been involved several times before."

"Will the parents be able to get them back?" I asked.

"That depends on if they follow the treatment plan or not. They are ordered to attend parenting classes, succumb to random drug tests, maintain a visitation schedule with the children and abide by all court rulings in this case," Linda answered.

"Are they doing that?" I inquired.

Linda's husband answered this time. "They struggle; when drugs and alcohol are involved, the return rate of children to their homes goes way down."

Just then the back door flew open, and all seven of them came running in. Marissa jumped in my lap and informed me she was going to stay there until we finished talking. The other kids continued to play. I noticed they had become a little overly excited for the living room. "Well, we should probably go now," I interjected.

In unison they answered, "No."

Our kids said they wanted to stay; the other kids asked us not to go. They began hugging us around our waists and begging and pleading. They even gave us a choice, either not to go, or to go and take them with us. It was a truly wonderful feeling to be wanted this much by a child. I knew it was odd they had taken to us so quickly. Against our better judgment, and against what we had asked of them, they continued to call us Mom and Dad. It felt wrong, but the truth is, we had no experience; so we thought this could be normal for kids with their background.

"We have to go now," Joe said, "but we will see you again."

I knew they did not believe that for a moment, because when they heard those words they headed out to the back-yard again, as if somehow they knew it was not going to happen. It made me so sad; it made all of us sad. We said our good-byes to the foster parents and told them we would talk it over and get back to Louis about our decision. They nodded and looked at us as if they knew they would never see us again.

As we were leaving, the foster mom called me aside. "Just so you know, they have been in placement for fifty-seven days. They were placed in our intake home for thirty days and have been given one extension of an additional thirty days to find a more permanent placement. If a home is not found for them within the next three days, they will have to be separated; they cannot stay here or in intake forever."

I looked at her wondering how I could possibly process this new information.

When we arrived home, the kids were too excited to sleep. Joe and I were equally excited. I realized we had not even eaten dinner before we went to visit because the kids had been in such a hurry to leave. I made a snack for all of us, and we sat around the kitchen table discussing what seemed surreal.

"If we allowed them to stay with us, where would they sleep? We don't have room for three more children," Joe began.

"I will share my room," Joey exclaimed, "because Colton and I are the same age."

"I will too," Amanda continued.

"Me too," Paul chimed in, "because Willy and I are the same age."

It was true—all three of them were almost the same ages as our children. I could not help but wonder if that was a good thing or not.

I looked at Amy. "I would like to have Marissa as my friend. I would like to share a room with her," she said softly.

We assured them there would be many sacrifices. They would all have to share their rooms, their toys, their books and even the time they spent with us. This would change their entire childhoods. We might as well have been talking to ourselves; I do not think they heard a word. They had made up their minds, and there was no going back. I knew Joe and I would need to be the voices of reason here. We would need to talk after we put them to bed.

There was no denying this was not what we had envisioned. We had simply wanted to take in one child and give him the opportunities he would not otherwise be afforded. Neither Joe nor I felt equipped to commit to this. Yet one thing continued to haunt me. When I first saw the children, it was not as if I was seeing strangers. I had an immediate sense of recognition. I somehow knew them, because my first response, although silent to others, was, "Oh, there you are." I know that sounds strange; I knew then that most people would not understand. Still, I felt this was what we had been called to. I knew that, despite my misgivings, this was to be.

To my surprise, Joe felt exactly the same way, maybe not the sense of recognition, but certainly that this was meant to be. He needed no convincing; in fact, I think he was surprised he did not need to convince me. There it was; we made the decision, although I am equally sure everyone would say there was no real decision.

In the morning we called Louis and told him we would go forward with the process of taking in the children. He told us the next step would be to bring the kids over to our house for a sleepover the following night. It was all moving so incredibly fast. Even though we had decided to do this, I am not sure we had processed it yet or that even one of us truly understood the implications of such a decision. I know, for myself at least, I tried to occupy my mind with the immediate thoughts of how to prepare for the big sleepover instead of how to prepare for our new life.

We purchased four sets of bunk beds to replace the single beds in each of the children's rooms, as well as new dressers to accommodate their belongings. We also bought each of them a new desk, filled with everything they would need for school. Then we picked out a special stuffed animal to be waiting on each of their beds when they arrived. We held off on buying their bedding; we thought it would be best if the kids could pick out their own sheets and comforters to make the bed feel more like their own.

We picked Colton, Marissa and Willy up the following afternoon. They had their clothes packed and were waiting by the front door. They were so excited to see us, but we were equally excited to see them. First, we took them shopping to pick out what they needed for their rooms. They were well behaved, polite and extremely thankful for everything. They were hugging me as I was standing in line at the cashier. Suddenly Marissa darted over to the magazine rack in the next aisle. The provocative photo on the front of the maga-zine showed a beautiful woman wearing a very revealing dress. Marissa pointed to her breasts and called out, "Wow! Look at those boobs. I want some like that too." Then she walked back to me, put her arm around me and became that perfect little girl again.

When we arrived home, the children played as I began cooking dinner. I made fried chicken, mashed potatoes, home-made rolls, vegetables and pie. It was such a blessing to see how much the children loved it. I could not believe how much they ate and how much milk they drank. They kept asking for more; I wondered if it was to see if we would ever say no. We never did, and it was a dinner they would remember even years later.

The rest of the night was spent laughing, playing and getting to know one another. The transition seemed so easy that it gave us confidence in the fact that we could do this. We tucked them in, prayed with them—although they seemed very confused by that gesture—kissed them good night and then snuggled them in tight in their blankets. Joe and I went into their rooms several more times, just to look at them and envision what the future would hold. We felt blessed that God entrusted us with these beautiful children, if only for a short time.

As much as we enjoyed them, we understood their stay with us might be brief. In a strange twist, we understood that if the best were to happen to them their stay with us would be brief. They needed their parents. Colton, Marissa and Willy had lived with their biological mother since birth. Colton and Marissa had no real recollection of their biological father; he had left the family early on. Willy's biological father then became the stepfather to both Colton and Marissa. We did not know much of the family history, but we did know that in general the best place for a child is with his or her birth family.

Until that could happen we would gladly nurture and care for these beautiful children. They had breakfast with us the following morning and played outside with Mandy, Joey,

Amy and Paul. Before we knew it, the time had come to take them back to their foster home.

They cried when we dropped them off, even though we assured them that in only a couple of days we would be back to take them home with us to live. When we did return they seemed surprised we had kept our word. We became an instant family; I could not help but notice there was such innocence about us. Just as with our children, Marissa, Colton and Willy loved to snuggle and hug; we did a lot of that. I do not think there was ever a time when I sat down that one or more of them did not jump in my lap. Often all the furniture in the room would be empty except the couch we were all sitting on—with Joe and me, our children and now them cuddled up together like a litter of puppies. It seemed as if we could not get close enough.

We were blessed in that we had never experienced sibling rivalry between our children; they had always treated each other with respect and genuine love, which did not change with the addition of three more. They played, they laughed and they listened to each other's stories, with the absolute confidence we had all made the right decision.

We now had seven children, and even though this meant a lot of laundry, a lot of cooking and a lot of scraped knees to mend and tears to kiss, it was a gift beyond measure.

Chapter Two

The Early Years

~~~~~~~~~~~~~~~~~~~~~~~~~~~~~~~~~~~~~

Psalm 100:2
"Worship the Lord with gladness;
come before
him with joyful songs."

~~~~~~~~~~~~~~~~~~~~~~~~~~~~~~~~~~~~~

Those were fond memories and inspired me to begin the long process of clearing out the debris from the porch. I swept up piles of leaves and remnants of an existence I barely remembered. How had I let it get this bad? I looked over at the clay pots outlining the porch. I was startled to notice the flowers seemed to have died in full bloom. The vines, leaves and even buds were brownish in color and brittle; yet they stood in perfect replication of how they had that last summer. It was as if they blossomed one moment and found death in the next. I was haunted by that vision because it so paralleled my life. I sat back down and continued the painful journey of remembering the defining moments that had caused my own frailty.

We filled the next few weeks with getting Colton, Marissa and Willy enrolled in the elementary school our children attended, meeting with their caseworker and arranging therapy, as well as family visitation. Social Services decided the children would have unsupervised visitation with their mother every Saturday from 10:00 a.m. until 5:00 p.m. We were responsible for driving them to the county building where their mother would then meet us. She would have them for the day and then return them to Social Services in the afternoon, where we would pick them up.

As for therapy, the county requested the usual testing. Colton and Marissa were administered an IQ test; the results were extremely low. The therapist was concerned they would struggle severely in school. The other tests appeared to be more encouraging, noting no real problems. Nevertheless, we scheduled weekly therapy to help the children deal with the loss they must surely be feeling about leaving their home and family.

I was concerned because I never saw any of this emotion from Colton or Marissa. I never once saw them cry a tear over missing either their mother or their father. Both Joe and I questioned them repeatedly about how they were feeling. The answer was always the same. "We don't miss them. We're glad we don't have to live there anymore, and we get to live with you guys instead." We knew this was not likely their actual feelings but thought perhaps they were in the denial stage of their grief and that through therapy would be better able to access their deeper feelings. William was able to show sadness; this offered us the opportunity to tend to his needs.

Colton and Marissa spoke negatively of their past; they told story after story of the abuse and neglect they had endured. They spoke of always being hungry and no one meeting their needs. This most adversely affected Colton. He once told us, in tears, that he felt bad because he and Marissa were so hungry they went to a 7-11 store and stole a bag of spaghetti.

He went on to say they would take the spaghetti and break off pieces, eating it dry and always sparingly. He said he knew that stealing was wrong, but when he was hungry, he had no choice. That incident, and one in which he stole some chocolate syrup, seemed to really bother him.

More poignantly, he told of a story when he had eaten a handful of pennies. He had been so angry at being hungry again that he decided if he ate the pennies, they would stay in his stomach and he would never again feel hunger. He was taken to the hospital after that.

It was odd because the impulse that most of us have to eat if we are hungry Colton did not possess. When he got hungry, he got angry. I had to remind him to eat; it was not a natural response for him. I watched him repeatedly go to the cabinets or the refrigerator and just look in. He did not overeat; he just needed to be assured there was enough food if he got hungry. He would even bring snacks to school to keep in his desk. His teacher said he rarely ate them but became very anxious if he did not have them.

Marissa was not angry about food or about anything for that matter, or if she was, she never showed it. She seemed very guarded; it was almost as if she did not allow herself the luxury of being upset. It did not matter what happened to her—she put a smile on her face and assured everyone around her she was fine.

I remember shortly after she started school a little girl from her class invited her to a birthday party. Marissa was so excited; she said it was her very first birthday party. We went out and bought the perfect dress for her to wear and the perfect present for this little girl. I was almost as excited as she was; I was happy for her. It was all we talked about the next week.

Unfortunately, on the morning of the party, I received a phone call from this girl's mother. She said that her daughter had been behaving badly and she had made the decision to cancel the party. I thought it was a terrible idea, not just for

Marissa, but also for her daughter and for the other girls who were planning to attend; but it was not my decision to make. Nevertheless, it was distressing, and I was hesitant to tell Marissa. When she returned from school, ready to change and head to her very first birthday party, I told her what happened.

"Um," she said, "I did not want to go anyway. I would rather stay here with you."

I tried to get her to reveal her true feelings; I reminded her it was okay to feel bad when something bad happened. She assured me she never felt bad.

Soon after, I finally did see some true emotion. It was Halloween; I was not sure how, or if, the kids had celebrated this holiday in the past so I wanted to make it special. I took all seven of the children to a local indoor amusement park for the day. We spent the entire day, riding rides, eating pizza and playing games. It was late afternoon before we headed back home to prepare for Halloween night. I expected the children to be so happy; I had purchased new costumes for them, and Marissa's was a little angel. As I was getting her dressed, she began to cry.

"What's wrong?" I asked in concern.

"I don't want to go," she said between sobs.

"Why don't you want to go?" I asked. "It should be a lot of fun."

"No, I have gone door-to-door and asked for food before; it was not fun."

At that moment I realized her perception of absolutely everything was different from ours. We needed to be much more careful in the future about looking at situations from different angles.

As for Willy, it was tough to know what was really going on with him; he was so very difficult to understand. I remember once he asked me for a "dutie." When I did not know what he meant, he became more and more frustrated. I tried to give him water, juice, even a piece of fruit; he wanted none of it. Finally I said, "Willy, you have to show me what a 'dutie' is because I don't know." He went across the kitchen and pointed up to the counter on which sat the cookie jar.

"Oh." I sighed. "A dutie is a cookie."

I wondered then if his speech difficulty had something to do with his not hearing properly. We took him to have his hearing tested; sure enough, that was the problem. The doctor said that due to a series of untreated ear infections scar tissue had formed, thus dramatically compromising his hearing. He gave us a prescription for an antibiotic, a yummy pink, bubble-gum flavored liquid. I will never forget how happy Willy was when we went to the pharmacy to pick it up. They put it in a small white paper sack and folded over the top. I handed it to Willy; he held it by the top so carefully and could not stop smiling. "My meecine," he said repeatedly.

Willy went through a series of three operations on his ears and one operation to remove his adenoids. These were difficult to schedule because there was some opposition from his mom; but eventually Social Services intervened and authorized the surgeries. Further, since there was no record of Willy receiving any immunizations, we had no choice but to have the complete list of childhood shots administered. This meant a series of about four injections per visit over a several month period. Willy was never quite as excited about going to the doctor again.

We were pleased his hearing began showing improvement; but his development was severely delayed. We decided to have him tested at an early intervention program for at-risk children. We were fortunate; they accepted Willy into a preschool program designed to help him with his speech.

The only real behavior problem we experienced with Willy was his stealing. This little four-year-old boy stole from every place he ever went. We had to go back into stores to return merchandise; we had to return to friends' houses to give back the items he had taken. Once in therapy I was expressing my frustration to the therapist about my inability to deter this behavior. While I was speaking, she looked around me to see Willy stuffing a silver bank she had sitting on her shelf down his pants.

She asked Willy to give it back and then allowed him to go play while we talked. She assured me this was a common trait of children with histories of long-term neglect and unmet needs. She went on to say that if a child believes he or she will not get from others what they need, they decide to go and get it for themselves. Finally, she said, as soon as Willy felt his needs were being met, this behavior would cease. It would take months, but she was right—the stealing did stop.

Colton displayed no real behavior problems, except for his anger, but he did display some behavior that concerned us. The therapist at school informed us Colton had told all his teachers and his friends that he had been switched at birth and we had finally found him, our biological son; he was not adopted. Colton was adamant on this point, and once, when I asked him about it in therapy, he seemed for a moment confused as to that not being the truth.

At night he would often sleepwalk. The therapist explained to us that this was one symptom of post-traumatic stress disorder. This would be concerning enough, but it was coupled with the fact that while he was sleepwalking he would urinate in different places in the house, perhaps thinking he was in the bathroom. Once in the toy box, once in the closet and once he began to urinate on the easy chair Joe was then sitting in. Joe called out to him to stop, but Colton was obviously not awake.

As with Willy, we were assured this behavior would end, and as soon as Colton felt safe, he would begin sleeping through the nights. This too took time, but in the end Colton began sleeping much better; it was the daytime behavior that then concerned us.

Joe bought each of the children a brand new bike, unaware that neither Colton, Marissa nor Willy had any idea how to ride. Joe, along with my brother, spent an entire day, until the sun went down, teaching them. After that, we could never get Colton off a bike again; it was his newfound freedom. One day I looked out and saw he had a giant weed, about four feet in height, tied upright to the seat of his bike with a bungee cord. He was riding up and down the cul-de-sac talking to this weed.

Concerned, I went out and asked, "Colton, who are you talking to?"

"I am talking to Tony," he replied.

"Who is Tony?" I asked as I looked around.

With that, Colton turned to the weed, pointed and said, "This is Tony."

I was confused. "Where did you find Tony?"

Colton replied, "I found him in the backyard. In the daytime he can come with me and play, and at night I am going to plant him outside my room so he can watch the window and make sure no one can get in and steal me. He will protect me."

Unfortunately, not just Colton but the other children were often frightened that someone would try to take them, and they always seemed to seek some form of protection. We finally were able to put Tony to rest when we bought Colton a turtle that we then named Tony. He became the new protector.

In time the children began to complain about having to go to visitation each Saturday. They would say they were afraid, and that their mom would often leave them alone and hungry on these visits. We reported each of these allegations to Social Services, but it was their opinion it was in the best interest of the children to continue visitation.

Colton was becoming more and more agitated about these meetings, and one weekend, as we pulled up beside his mother, he refused to go. She put her hands around his arms and physically put him into the van. I worried about him the entire day. To compound that worry, his mother was two hours late bringing him and the other two back so we waited in the parking lot, imagining all sorts of horrible things. Little did we know how close our imagination was to reality.

A few weeks later, after the children attended their weekly visitation, they were noticeably quiet when they returned home. Willy seemed to need a few extra hugs and eventually fell asleep in my lap. I did not want to wake him so I laid him in his bed with his clothes still on. The following morning I ran the bath water; but when I lifted up Willy's shirt, to my astonishment I saw probably ten to twelve open wounds. They were circular and appeared to be burns.

"What happened?" I exclaimed.

He did not answer; instead, he began to cry. I asked again; again, no answer. I pulled him up onto my lap and rocked him. Several minutes passed, and then he said, "She called me 'Willy Will,' and that is what you call me. I told her only my real mom could call me that and so she got mad and burned me with her cigarette."

I was shocked and horrified. I called the caseworker, and she told me to take him to Children's Hospital immediately. I was apprehensive; the hospital was in downtown Denver, and I did not know my way. Joe was at work, but still I knew I needed to do this.

The doctor saw us quickly; he asked Willy nothing. After a thorough examination, he looked at me and said, "These are cigarette burns." He measured the circumference and diameter of the wounds and then showed me the depth of the burn, deepest in the center of the circle, the way a cigarette burns. "No doubt," he continued, "this child has been repeatedly burned." He went on to say he would file a report and of course be willing to testify, but I needed to take Willy to the police station and fill out a report.

As Willy and I left, I tried to explain to him, as much as anyone could, that he would have to tell the police officer what happened. I am not sure if he knew the impact this would have on his mother, but he agreed. He was so brave. The officer had a good deal of difficulty trying to understand Willy but was eventually able to get the information he needed.

Social Services cancelled all further visitations between the children and their biological family. The children acted very excited, but I wondered if deep down they were saddened. After their mom failed several urine tests and moved, leaving no forwarding address, the department decided to seek termination of parental rights. A court date was scheduled, and we were assigned a CASA, Gabby, to aid the children. A CASA is a Court Appointed Special Advocate who advocates for and provides services to child victims of abuse and neglect. She was kind to them; she took them to the movies and out to eat. She made her interviews fun for the kids, and they liked being tape-recorded.

Further, Gabby made it her personal mission to locate their mom and have her served with the arrest warrant. The police had given up on finding her, but Gabby, on her own time and through a period of personal crisis, did find her. Gabby then arranged for police intervention, and their mom was arrested. She denied the charges but after being incarcerated for a time did plead guilty. Termination of parental rights was granted, and the children were available for adoption.

Two years had now passed since the first day we met these children. We had been through some difficult times and some extremely joyful times. One of my most joyful moments was the day I first told Marissa about Jesus. We were sitting on the floor together; she was eating a bag of Skittles when I told her the whole story. She knew nothing of His birth, His life, His ministry or even His death. Months later, when the children were baptized, she was asked how she came to know the Lord. She smiled and said, "Over a bag of Skittles with my mom." Everyone in the congregation laughed, but I knew that moment was engrained in my heart forever.

The truth is each day was filled with such joy; we did so many silly things. Once I took the hose and sprayed down the entire hill behind our home for hours until it became a giant mudslide. Then, along with their friends, the children put on their bathing suits and spent the day sliding down the hill. It was comical because all I could see were the whites of their eyes; everything else was covered in mud.

I had as much fun as they did. They taught me to roller blade and play street hockey. I taught them to love old rock 'n' roll music, and we played it loud as we danced. Joe even built a giant clubhouse in the backyard, and they were able to sleep out there on warm summer nights. One of the children's favorite things to do was "Jammy Day." We usually had "Jammy Day" when it was cold, dark and snowy outside. We would stay in our pajamas all day long, drink hot chocolate, play board games and watch movies. Sometimes I think they enjoyed that as much as the elaborate birthday parties and holidays we celebrated. It did not matter what we were doing—we genuinely had fun.

So, when they became available for adoption, there were no doubts; we knew we wanted them as part of our family forever, and they wanted it as well. We invited everyone we knew. The children dressed in their best clothes—suits and ties and fancy dresses—and after the court proceeding, which was packed, we had a party. Friends, family and even their teachers attended; we were so happy. We had a big cake with a giant rainbow on it. I always told the children the rainbow in my life was missing a few colors—until they came—and now my rainbow was complete. They received many presents, which they gladly shared with their new brothers and sisters, and many hugs and welcoming hearts; it was a good day.

That night, as we were sitting around talking about all that had happened, Colton began laughing aloud. His silliness made us laugh although we had no idea why.

"What is so funny?" Joe finally asked.

"Remember those houses they said I had started a fire in and burned down?"

"Yes, I remember," I answered.

"Well, you know how I said I did not do it, that they just made that up to get me in trouble?"

"Yes," I answered again, this time more hesitantly.

He laughed again then said, "I did do it; I just didn't want to tell you at first because I wanted you to adopt me."

I had to catch my breath. Colton had been accused of starting a fire in two separate houses, each of which turned into a very serious situation. His parents had always claimed he did it. He claimed they were doing drugs and they did it.

"Colton, why would you start the house on fire?" I asked.

"I wanted help so bad. I thought if the house was on fire, the firefighters would have to come, and they would see we needed help and would take us. They came, but they did not take us."

"So, Colton, are we in any danger of your starting a fire here?" Joe asked.

"No, Dad, I don't need help here. I won't start any more fires."

Joe and I were concerned. Colton was so happy and so proud of the fact that he had kept his secret for so long; but he also seemed relieved to have finally told it. We were blessed and excited about such a wonderful day, but we could not help but wonder if there were not more secrets.

Chapter Three

More Decisions

~~~~~~~~~~~~~~~~~~~~~~~~~~~~~~~~~~~~~~~

2 Peter 3:18
"But grow in the grace
and knowledge
of our Lord and Savior Jesus Christ.
To him be glory
both now and forever!
Amen."

~~~~~~~~~~~~~~~~~~~~~~~~~~~~~~~~~~~~~~~

As the warm sun rose even higher on my day of discovery I felt hope for the first time. I reached into the woven bamboo basket and pulled out the wind chimes that once hung so proudly. Oddly enough they were not even dusty, preserved as if they had no idea of why they had lain hidden so long. I hung them up, and with the first wind, I remembered the joy they once brought. Nevertheless, there was a reason they had been put away; I needed to find the strength to remember.

Those first years after we adopted were truly happy and left our hearts open to go further with this ministry. One afternoon I was looking through the monthly mailer from Social Services when I came upon an ad for an extremely hard-to-place young girl. This caught my eye because Joe and I had always agreed we wanted to take in only children no one else wanted.

This girl was from Korea, she was eleven years old, and her family no longer lived in this country. That was all the information that was provided. When Joe came home we talked it over and decided to make the call to her caseworker.

"She is twelve now," her caseworker offered.

"How did she come to be in your custody?" I asked.

"It is a sad story. Her mother had taken her to the doctor because she was not feeling well. The doctor determined she was pregnant and of course made his report to our agency," she responded.

"I don't understand; is she pregnant?"

"No, the truth is she had been sexually abused for years by her father, and it was his," she continued.

"It," I repeated. I was offended by the word. "Where is 'it' now?"

"She had an abortion shortly after she came into our custody. We all felt it was the right thing for her. She was too young, eleven at the time, and her body was not mature enough; on top of that it was a product of incest, and we did not even know if it would be normal," she said with a matter-of-fact attitude.

"Did she make the choice for herself, or did you make it for her?"

"She needed guidance and support; that was our job, and we provided it. She had no one else. After the pregnancy was discovered and we took custody, the police went back to the apartment to arrest the father. The entire apartment had been cleaned out except for a few papers left lying on the floor. The father, mother and even her only brother had gone back to

Korea to avoid prosecution. They did not leave her so much as a note; she was abandoned. We placed her in an intake home and proceeded to address her medical concerns."

I could sense this woman was growing impatient with me, but I needed to stay on this subject just one more minute. "Did she make this decision, or did you?" I asked one more time.

"Listen—she made the decision as much as any eleven year old can make such a decision," she said sharply.

I knew the subject was closed.

"Besides all this mess," the caseworker continued, "she does well in school, has no real behavior problems and has been doing fine in placement."

"Amazing," I replied, "considering all she has been through."

"Are you still interested?" she hurriedly asked.

"Yes, I need to talk it over in more depth with my family, but I am interested," I assured her. "You will hear from us tomorrow."

Joe and I spoke first. Our hearts were truly open to this young person, but we were not sure how we would approach this with the children. This was a tragic story, some of which the older ones would be able to understand, but the younger ones would not. We had to make the decision whether or not to expose them to this kind of situation at such an early age.

Finally we agreed. This young girl had been abused and then abandoned by her family; alone in this country she needed someone. She needed to get out of intake, which is a short-term placement, and get into a home; we wanted to take her in.

We called the children in for a family meeting and tried to present it without the graphic details. As we had anticipated, the older ones did understand, and they were disgusted. The younger ones, even though it was evident they did not truly understand, did not ask many questions. They all were stuck on only one point. She had no family, and she needed one; we should take her in.

That night we all prayed together as a family. We prayed for the strength, the patience and the love it would take to make this young girl feel welcome in our home. In the morning I called the caseworker; to my surprise, she said she would bring Shin over that afternoon.

I responded, "I thought we would do some visits first and then bring her into the family slowly like we did with the other children."

"Oh, no, we don't really have that kind of time in this case; besides you already know everything about her. I will pack up her things, and we will be over before dinner."

I had not been prepared to hear that. I called Joe at work and explained the situation. "Well," he said, "then I guess she was meant to come today. I will try to get off work early, and we can all have a nice dinner together."

I had so much to do before she came. I wanted to prepare a room for her, make her bed, put out some things she might like; I wanted to make it special. It seems I had only gotten started when a car drove up outside. It was Shin and the foster woman with whom she had been staying. The woman drove up to the front of our home and let Shin out. When I looked out the window, Shin was trying to get her bag of clothes from the backseat. I ran out the front door. The foster mom was still sitting in the driver seat of the car, looking straight out the front window, as if she could not see Shin or me.

"Hello," I said. "I am Debbie." I looked at Shin as I said this. She was nothing as I had imagined. She was tall, almost as tall as I was. She certainly did not look eleven or even twelve. She was thin, very thin; she wore glasses, and it was quite evident she would need extensive work on her teeth. She was definitely at that awkward stage, which we each go through, but still she had a subtle beauty about her.

There was no response to my greeting from either of them. I shrugged a bit not understanding what was going on, and then I picked up the bag with which Shin had been struggling.

The foster mom reached over to the passenger seat, closed the door and said her only words: "See ya."

Shin and I were left standing on the curb with a white plastic garbage bag containing all she owned in this world. I was quiet for a moment; I had never envisioned our first meeting going like this. I smiled, put my arm on her back and said, "Come on. Let's go in the house."

She pulled away when I touched her; I had to remind myself not to do that again. This girl had been through so much, and I was sure the last thing she wanted was a stranger touching her.

When we came into the living room, I glanced at the clock. It was only about 1:00; no wonder I had not finished preparing for her arrival.

"Come and sit on the sofa," I coaxed. "Can I get you something to eat or drink? Have you had lunch?"

"I am not hungry," she said so softly.

These were the first words she had spoken. She seemed shy and maybe even afraid of me. I tried to make pleasant conversation, but nothing seemed to work. I remember feeling so awkward. I kept looking at the hands on the clock, longing for them to move faster so the kids would get home from school sooner. She answered all my questions with only one or two words and did not seek, on her part, for this conversation to continue. It was unmistakable; she felt as awkward as I did.

Finally there was an end. The front door swung open, and seven loud, laughing, energetic children bolted through the door. When they reached the top of the stairs, their "Hey, Mom, we're home" was interrupted by the sight of Shin sitting on the couch.

"Who are you?" Colton asked.

"Shin," she responded even quieter than before.

"I didn't think you would be so big," Marissa quipped.

'That's okay," Amanda said, jumping in. "You're more my size. Come on. Let's go get a snack."

With that, all of the children headed into the kitchen. I stayed in the living room because I wanted to give them a few minutes alone. I listened at the kitchen door and could hear that Shin was beginning to open up to them. She said more in those few minutes than she had said to me all afternoon.

They spent the next few hours getting to know each other; they even went outside to play as I began preparing dinner.

Every child is different, but that difference is certainly magnified when children are from different countries and thus different cultures. I did not previously know much about the Korean culture, and so I had much to learn from Shin. She took me to a Korean grocery store where her favorite items for purchase were seaweed and octopus. She made her favorite dinner for the entire family, and we each tried all of the dishes and even enjoyed them. Shin was proud of her heritage—rightly so—and it was fun for us to share different experiences with her.

The most difficult aspect of her adaptation to our family was that I was typically the disciplinarian. Joe worked all day, and when he got home he liked to play with the kids. He obviously was involved in all serious situations, but the day-to-day routines were my responsibility. Shin had been raised in an environment in which the father had absolute authority and the mother was subservient in attitude and action; this was quite different from our household. I made decisions regarding the children on a regular basis, and Joe generally agreed with them; if he did not, he did not show it in front of the children. Instead we talked about it alone and together came up with a better solution. I valued his opinion and realized at times it was an improvement over mine; but still I had one.

This was a complicated view for Shin to accept. She willingly accepted any consequence Joe deemed necessary to bestow on her; but if she had any inclination I had persuaded him to act in that manner, she rebelled against it. Shin was not oblivious to her actions. We talked about this openly and honestly. She sincerely did not feel that based on her beliefs and experiences I had any right or power, as a woman, to make decisions that affected other people's lives. This was often a point of contention between us.

When Joe was not home, Shin acted in a particular way. When Joe would return, her behavior would suddenly improve to that of the perfect daughter. Shin's relationship with her biological father was so dysfunctional that, in many ways, she did not know how to relate to Joe except from a point of absolute submission. Due to everything Shin had endured, Joe did not feel comfortable treating her the same way he did the other children. He could tickle, wrestle, and play roughly with them, but those were actions he thought would alienate Shin. Instead they took long walks and talked about life, during which times Shin remained guarded.

She obviously suffered from post-traumatic stress disorder and from the severe effects of abandonment. She obediently followed rules; she never directly defied or refused to comply with anything that was asked of her. Nonetheless it was obvious to us this submission was based on her fear and trepidation of the consequences, not on her feelings of love or respect for us.

My most vivid memory of Shin is that she often slept with her eyes open. I would go in at night to check on her, and she would be sound asleep, sometimes even snoring, but with her eyes wide open. She slept very lightly and was easily startled. It was easy for anyone to see she was a child of serious trauma, but she was so very hard to reach.

I tried to talk to her about her family. She was protective of her secrets, perhaps because of shame and embarrassment or perhaps out of true love and loyalty for her family; she always spoke fondly of them. She clearly had a deep love for both her parents and her brother. She spoke of happy times and warm memories; she missed them unbelievably.

Adopting Shin was not an option. Her parents had left the country before their parental rights had been terminated; she was not legally free. Even if she were, I am not sure this would have been a consideration for either her or us. We definitely had our reservations, but she had a tremendous loyalty to her family and her heritage. We all understood this was a foster placement.

I was startled once when she came down the stairs wearing her father's pajama bottoms. I could not understand why she would wear the pants of the man who had incestuously raped her on numerous occasions. I asked her about it, and she replied that wearing his clothes made her feel closer to him and she missed him. Not having endured this experience, I found it difficult to understand what she was really going through.

Shin and I did not have a bad relationship; we had a relationship of mutual misunderstanding. We viewed the world differently, and even though we both cared for each other, there was this barrier between us. Not so between Joe and Shin. She not only obeyed him, but she also seemed to like him and, in time, grew to respect and admire him. In the end, though, she would rebel against even his rules.

As she grew, so too did our struggles with her. She was constantly stealing, even taking the presents from under the Christmas tree to sell. She got on the bus each morning, but many times, she did not go to school. She became more and more secretive. We often wondered if we were the right home for her. We even wondered what the right home for her would look like. She made some movement toward us, but at the same time, she made equal movements away from us. We continued with individual and family therapy and awaited a future we could not predict.

At about that time we received another call from Social Services. They had in their custody a young girl named Shelby. They needed immediate placement for Shelby and asked us to come in within the hour to pick her up. We had not considered more children, but as before, we went blindly in faith.

We were nervous when we arrived at the county building and were being led up to the room Shelby was in. But when we entered and saw her, we had no feelings except for complete excitement and joy.

She was beautiful. She had the longest brown curly hair, chubby cheeks and a smile that embraced and held us. I sat down by her and looked into her eyes, not believing her incredible beauty. She lifted both her hands, placed them on my cheeks and pulled my face into hers.

"Hey, you look like me." Those were the first words she spoke to me. Her caseworker then spent some time telling us about her story and the fact that she was three and had a brother Benjamin who was four and was in placement as well. She spoke in detail, but she did not have my attention. I was too focused on Shelby and her on me.

When the meeting was finished and the caseworker told us to take her home, I felt as if I had been given the greatest gift of my life. I picked her up, and she clung to me. We were instantly in love; Joe went to get the car, and Shelby and I never took our eyes off each other. Even on the drive home I looked back at her in her car seat the entire way; she was beautiful.

The children adored her, as did Joe, that is, in the little time they had together; I did not want to share her with anyone. Shelby and I did everything together. She would sit on the counter and help me make dinner, and she followed me around, helping me do laundry and the daily chores. Her favorite time was bath time. She was insistent on wearing the same powder and perfume I did, and then she would crawl into bed with me for her story and hugs before prayers. After the struggles with Shin and her absolute inability to bond with me, it was so fulfilling to have Shelby who genuinely chose me.

We even took Shelby to visit with her brother, Benjamin, and had him over to the house on several occasions. It was important to keep a bond between them, as of course the entire goal would be to reunite them in a permanent placement. We accepted the fact that if we kept Shelby that would mean keeping Benjamin, and so it would be imperative for us to develop a relationship with him. We did develop a relationship, and even though it was not as deep as the one with Shelby, that was attributed entirely to the fact that we did not have as much time with him. The time we did have, we truly cherished.

We were so happy; the days were filled with a sense of genuine joy, joy that had been missing. Short of the fact that Joe was beginning to feel a little left out by my closeness to Shelby and the amount of time we spent together, everything was perfect. For the next few months we were so happy; Shelby was the ideal ending to this journey.

We still struggled with Shin, though. One night, angry that she had to spend time studying because of her grades, she ran away. I panicked when I went to her room and saw she was gone; but I knew if I showed her that, then I would give her behavior power and control. I believed in my heart that she "ran" for attention and did not intend to stay gone. I did not want the other children to be upset by or somehow modeled to by this behavior.

Joe and I decided to call the police, make a report and then take the children out to dinner and a movie so they would not be alarmed. I acted as if everything was fine, but I cannot even remember the movie we saw; I was anxious and praying for her safety. When we returned home the house was still dark, but I noticed the screen in the kitchen window had been cut and some things were missing from the house. We made sure the other kids did not notice as we tucked them in.

About midnight the doorbell began ringing continuously. At first Joe and I decided to ignore it, but it became evident that whoever it was would not leave. Joe went to the door. Outside stood Shin holding the items she had taken from the house. Joe opened the door as Shin sobbingly asked if she could come back in. At that time I walked into the room, and the three of us sat down and decided where to go from there.

After much discussion on our part and many tears on Shin's, we decided we would write a contract. The contract would state that as long as Shin obeyed the rules of the house, foremost being not to run away, she would be allowed to stay with us. If she left again, she would need to leave our home permanently. This was a deal breaker; in a home with so many children we could in no way encourage this behavior.

Shin agreed, and we sat until the wee hours of the morning discussing, writing and signing this contract. By morning we called the police to let them know she was safe and had returned the stolen items and then tucked Shin safely back in bed.

Unfortunately this was only the beginning of some very tough behavior. Within a couple of weeks I received a phone call from the principal of the high school Shin was attending. He informed me Shin was in his office after being caught stealing items from the gym lockers. He went on to say that Shin had recently begun associating with a gang at the school and she had informed him that some of her behavior was part of the initiation. Finally he told us that when they searched Shin's locker they found many stolen items that had been missing from the school.

He put Shin on the phone, and I told her we would need to speak about this when she got home. But she did not come home. Again we called the police, and then we called Social

Services and assured them that when she did come home we were returning custody to them. We no longer had control over her behavior. Shin called late that evening and said she would be home shortly. We told her she could not come home and that she should call her caseworker.

Within minutes we received a call from that caseworker, from the loud music and noise she was apparently at either a party or a bar. She told us we would need to take Shin back because there was nowhere to place her. Again we reiterated that we had followed protocol in having her sign a contract and she had broken that contract; we were not taking her back. The caseworker became very angry, and some harsh words were exchanged. This situation had obviously, quite drastically, interrupted her evening. Finally she said in anger that she would be over the following afternoon to pick up Shin's things.

We knew the situation had not gone well, but we were sure that when the heat of the moment had passed the caseworker would understand we were following through with the natural consequence of her behavior, as well as setting an example for the other children. We could not have been more wrong.

The following day the caseworker did arrive, along with the news that the department was removing Shelby from our home because they had found another family for her, a family that would adopt both her and Benjamin. We were devastated. It was our intention to adopt both of them, and the county knew that. We loved them. We were left with the question of whether or not it was possible that because we did not allow Shin to return, we were punished by losing both Shelby and Benjamin. The county always claimed that was not true, that it was merely a coincidence; we could not help but believe it was. We did all we could—we made phone calls; we wrote letters—all to no avail. Within two weeks, Shelby was gone forever. We never saw either her or Benjamin again.

Further, after the many years Shin spent with our family, to our dismay, none of us ever heard from her again.

Chapter Four

Another White Trash Bag

Those memories drained the life from me. I sat back down on the rocking chair and tried to remember why I had thought it important to come out here. At this moment I was truly hesitant to go further. I rocked back and forth, overwhelmed with a sense of loss. My work of clearing this debris would have to wait for a little while; I would need to sit for these next memories and regain my strength.

I continued on. Within a two-week period we now had two fewer children in our home. We were very saddened by losing Shelby and decided to take this opportunity to rethink where we wanted to go. I did not want to give my heart to another child after Shelby left and Shin had been so difficult; this was a good time to take a hiatus. It was spring, and I looked forward to spending the summer with the children and just relaxing.

Amanda, Marissa and Amy went to Girl Scout horse-back riding camp and the boys to Boy Scout camp. We went bike riding, hiking and on picnics and had many adventures. The children collected snakes from the field and built forts in the backyard. We were constantly at the reservoir or the park. We loved the summer, and this one was just for us, or at least that was the plan.

Nevertheless, as with even the grandest of plans, they often go astray. The phone rang, and it was another foster mom who had taken in two boys, Cain, age eight, and Jonathon, age four. She ran an intake home, and the children were at the end of their time there. She was trying to help Social Services find a more permanent placement for these boys.

"Meet me at McDonald's in an hour, and you can meet them," she said as if she knew I would drop everything and come running, which of course I did — we did. Joe, I, and all the kids climbed into the van, and we headed off. After all, this was just a meeting; on top of it we could get the kids something for dinner, and I would not have to cook.

We pulled up to McDonald's and parked, and the kids started to climb out. A woman opened the van door next to us and said, "Hey, Joe and Deb, here they are."

We looked over and saw two boys. They both had shaven heads and tattered clothes. Next to them sat two white trash bags. *Oh, no,* I thought, *not again.*

"I brought all their belongings," the foster mom announced. "I was going to stay for dinner, but I'm late and have to run. Do you want me to help you get them into your van?"

I could not answer for a moment and then said with a stutter, "They are going…home with us tonight?"

"Sure. There's no need to do it any other way, but seriously I really do need to get going."

With that, she loaded the two white trash bags into our van and drove off. We stood quietly in the parking lot surrounded now by nine children and had no idea of what had just happened. Later they played in the play land, and Joe and I sat by ourselves at the table next to it. We spent the entire time trying to think of a way to make sense out of this in our minds. We already had seven children. We could not take two more when we had not even discussed it. And, after we did, Joe and I both agreed we just could not take in two more kids. Yet here they were.

We knew nothing of them. Johnny, the youngest one, displayed some rather disturbing behaviors. He would rock back and forth for long periods of time. He seemed to have periods of extreme happiness and periods of extreme sadness, during which he would not even speak. We were very concerned about his mental health.

We had a psychiatrist come to our house and evaluate him. She felt that most of his behavior was learned. Their mom, we were told, suffered considerably from mental illness before the children were removed from the home. The doctor assured us this was nothing to concern ourselves with, and we believed her. We had seen odd behavior from the other children when they were first placed with us, and we had also seen this behavior resolve.

Cain, the eight year old, did not concern us. His behavior, although I would classify it as a little rough and definitely "all boy," did not seem outside the realm of normality.

We put both boys in therapy and signed Cain up for school. Through therapy we learned the root of some of Johnny's odd behavior. For example, he would never come to us for anything; instead, he would get it himself. I could offer him a snack, and he would say no; but as soon as I left the room, he would go and take it. He accepted nothing; even if he was hurt he would not accept comfort from us. I remember once when he stubbed his toe on the living room table, screamed "damn!", and then laughed almost hysterically, even though it was evident he was in much pain. His reactions never matched his emotions, and he never allowed any of us as much as a hug. We finally did get a diagnosis; Johnny suffered from reactive attachment disorder.

We placed Johnny in a day treatment program where he worked with therapists at the same time as he went to preschool. He committed to this program and worked hard in therapy. He had a true desire to get better and be like "all the other kids." By the end of the school year he had made great progress. I was encouraged when, during therapy, Johnny asked to use the restroom. As he was leaving he accidentally shut his finger in the door. He ran to me, fell in my lap and cried as he allowed me to comfort him. He was considered a real success story and allowed to leave day treatment with the promise of normal kindergarten in the fall.

It had been a tough year. The Department of Social Services sought and the family court system granted termination of parental rights for both Cain and Johnny. As a family we made the decision that with the progress Johnny had made and his willingness to commit to therapy, along with the absence of any real problems with Cain, we would adopt them. Just as with the previous adoption it was a time of celebration and welcoming. We had struggled getting to this point and were all ready for a little lighthearted fun.

I signed the kids up for all kinds of summer activities; we had great fun. We would leave about 7:30 each morning, stop by the bakery and get a fresh bagel, banana and orange juice and then head to the track for practice until 10:00. Johnny used to run the track while hugging his teddy bear. We would then come home for a short rest, and then we had either swimming or tennis lessons, depending on the day. The kids all took golf lessons as well and played nine holes whenever they could. They also had baseball practice and endless games, which we all enjoyed. In our spare time we hung out at the pool; the kids loved to swim. It was a special summer. I even made up little books for each of the kids with pictures in them of all the fun things we did; they still have those books.

Unfortunately, somewhere in the middle of that summer, I started to notice some changes in Cain. I was not sure what was going on. I attributed some of it to the adoption only months earlier and the sense of finality he must be experiencing in his feelings for his biological family. I wanted to support him but at the same time allow him the opportunity and space to grieve. Still, it seemed as if there was something more. He once had gotten along so well with the other children, and now I sensed he was purposely isolating himself. His behavior became odd; there was nothing distinct, just odd.

His personal hygiene began to suffer; he refused to take a shower or even brush his teeth. Repeatedly he went into the bathroom, ran the water and then came back out promising he had taken a shower, even though it was evident he had not. His eating habits also began to change. I became concerned because he seemed to be eating less and less; his weight loss was becoming noticeable. I made an appointment with our pediatrician for a complete physical. She did a series of blood tests and a thorough examination. The diagnosis was that he was healthy, and even though his weight was low, she assured me it was within the normal range. I felt better.

The next afternoon I received a follow-up call from the doctor. She stated, "The blood tests are back, and they look fine. His glucose is a little low but, other than that, fine."

"That is good news," I said. "I am wondering, though, what would make his glucose low?"

"Oh, it is probably as simple as he had just not eaten before he came into the office," she assured me.

"No," I responded. "I made him French toast, bacon and juice before he came in. I watched him eat."

"Is it possible he is throwing up?"

I shook my head and then looked over at Cain. He was so thin and appeared so unhealthy to me. "I don't know. I will watch him more closely and follow up with you after I know more," I replied.

With that, I went into the kitchen and sat down at the table with Cain. I asked him if he had been sick lately, and he was adamant that he had not. Amanda came into the room at that time and contradicted what Cain had just said.

"Cain, I heard you in the bathroom the other night. You were throwing up. I've heard it more than once."

Cain denied this, saying only that it must have been someone else Amanda had heard. He would not admit to any problems with eating or being sick. But this became more and more an area of concern as his weight continued to decrease. Besides the hygiene issue and the eating problem, there was something else. It was hard to put into words; he just began acting weird. He started intentionally trying to embarrass his brothers and sisters; he acted out in ways to draw attention to himself, but the attention was always negative. There seemed to be no difference in his perception of negative and positive attention and even consequences.

As the summer progressed, so too did this new behavior. Cain increasingly became the focal point of the family meetings and was demanding more and more of us as a family. The other children, primarily Joey and Colton, were spending less and less time with him. It was odd, though, because Cain either did not notice or did not mind. I thought he was intentionally trying to set himself apart from the other children. They were all athletes; he made a point that he was not. He liked science and math and did not like sports. That did not matter to us; we were happy he had something he enjoyed, but it was a source of separation from the other kids. They all loved to eat, and they ate lots. Cain, it appeared, used food, or the lack thereof, as a weapon against himself. Whatever it was the other children enjoyed, Cain did not. He was truly becoming a loner.

As the summer ended and a new school year began, this behavior became apparent to others. At school Cain struggled socially. On the playground he did not have the skills to walk up to a child he did not know and ask that child to play. Instead he would sometimes spit on his hand and chase the other child around, threatening to touch him with his saliva. He was still able to get a response from the child, and even though it was negative, it seemed to be enough for him. Unfortunately it does not take long at this age, ten years old, for school children to determine who is and is not worthy of their mocking and ridicule. Cain, they determined, was, and he was continuously made fun of and teased.

Joe and I had never dealt with a situation like this before. The other children had always been popular, except for that brief time with Amy in preschool. She had a patch on one eye for a year, wore glasses and could not hear very well. That was easy, though. We just let her quit—she was only four. Unfortunately we could not do this with Cain. I tried role-playing at home. We worked through different scenarios of approaching kids at the playground or at lunch. I was sure that given the skills, which he quite obviously did not possess, he could become more socially acceptable. I was pleased with his desire and willingness to learn.

The children, however, were not as patient. They had begun to hear from the other kids at school about the weird behaviors of their brother, and they were distancing themselves from that behavior and reputation. It was becoming increasingly difficult to function as a complete family. It was the eight kids and then Cain. I wondered so often if he was not deliberately creating this role. He gave no outward signs that any of this bothered him.

Throughout the school year there was one problem after another. The school called me to come down on a regular basis, and each time Cain was adamant he had done nothing wrong. I know it is difficult for children to accept the concept of personal responsibility. It is a concept that needs to be taught, but Cain was unwilling to learn. He neither admitted to nor accepted responsibility for any of his actions. If he was caught doing something wrong, it was only because someone else had made him do it.

I found it very concerning when the school called and asked me to come down because another parent had an issue with Cain. When I arrived, I met with the teacher and the other parents. They told me Cain had repeatedly approached their daughter in the classroom and on the playground and even waited for her outside the restroom. She had attempted to deal with this herself; but despite her outward rejections of him, Cain was now stalking her, leaving her notes and threatening her. Her parents went on to say she no longer felt safe at school and they had failed in their efforts to convince her to return. I looked at the teacher and then the parents. I sighed. I was fully aware I could do nothing to make any of this better. I had no control over Cain, and even though that was extremely difficult to admit, I had to face the truth.

I was ill equipped to handle him or his behaviors. I tried the traditional discipline techniques I had used on the other children. I grounded him and took away his bike; I even made him write sentences. Nothing had an effect on Cain. He obviously did not mind when I sent him to his room; he enjoyed it because he liked not being expected to engage or interact with the family. I tried having him work for positive consequences—a party or having a friend over, for example—but he did not consider those things a reward. I continually worked to find something he would consider worthwhile, something that would merit a change in his behavior, but I could not.

He liked books, and I could have used this as a reward, except that this promoted isolation because he loved to lie on

his bed and read for hours by himself. I tried negative consequences such as losing privileges, but Cain did not seek
privileges anyway; he deprived himself of so many things.
Intentionally or not he was missing so much of life, and I had
no idea how to get him to reconnect.

Chapter Five

RAD

~~~~~~

James 5:15
"And the prayer offered in faith
will make the sick person well;
the Lord will raise him up.
If he has sinned,
he will be forgiven."

~~~~~~

I could not help but remember the confusion I felt at that time. I stood to stretch and walked over to the other end of the veranda. There, lying amidst the litter was a tiny dead bunny. It was not obvious what had happened to her. Maybe it was the cold, the lack of food or even another animal. I guess the reason does not matter; she did not survive. She would not see the beauty of what I was creating. She would not see the new young flowers, the birdbath bubbling with cool water or even the strawberries I was planting specially for the bunnies. Her life ended amidst confusion, chaos and neglect. It reminded me that to survive was all that mattered, for she would have had no way of knowing that if she had endured only a little longer, her life would have been so different. I continued to work and remember—because no matter how difficult this was, I had survived.

We of course were attending therapy with Cain, and the initial diagnosis was the same as Johnny's, reactive attachment disorder. I knew something about this particular disorder but was eager to learn more. I wanted to be able to reach Cain on his level. I wanted so much to be able to help him, in the same way we had helped Johnny. At one point we discussed some type of drug therapy; I was biased against this because of some recent articles I had read concerning foster and adopted children and the overwhelmingly disproportionate number of them that were prescribed drugs. My thinking, although naïve, was that drugs were just an easy answer and only masked, did not fix, the real problem. It was my goal to address the underlying issues, and so I refused to engage in any further discussions of medication.

Reactive attachment disorder, I learned, happens in the early years of a child's life. It was due, in this particular case, to the bond that was broken between Cain and his biological mother. From what I knew, Cain's mom was emotionally well at the time of his birth. Her health did not deteriorate until he was about four, so they had some good times between the two of them in the early years. At the onset of his mom's illness she was hospitalized a number of times, first for short periods and gradually longer and longer. Cain and his mother were separated on many occasions, but when Social Services finally intervened the bond was truly severed.

This part I understood; it made sense why he suffered from this disorder. Some of the symptoms were what you would expect from someone who had suffered from such a severe break in a mother/child relationship. Cain, as in other children who suffer from RAD, possessed an innate inability to trust others. He built a wall to protect himself from ever suffering that kind of hurt again. His inability to trust that he could survive another loss kept him from connecting with others.

This explained some of his behavior, and it was encouraging to understand the source of his pain. But it was discouraging to learn the prognosis was not great. In all likelihood Cain would never experience the depth of a truly loving and genuine relationship. This was heartbreaking. Still I had seen dramatic changes in Colton, Marissa and Willy. I had to remain confident that through the Lord all things are possible. Thus, despite what I knew, I remained optimistic that Cain would be one of the ones who made it.

I always felt this way, confident and assured; at least I always did while I was sitting in the therapist's office. It was only when I returned home I had to face that I had no idea what I was doing. Cain began stealing. I found out about this first from his school. They had caught him stealing from the lunch line numerous times. I tried several different approaches to deter this behavior; yet it continued. The stealing progressed from school to home. We thought money was missing on several different occasions. We never kept an exact count on the cash we had on hand so we were never certain, but we had the sense that it was. Then other items, some even from his brothers and sisters, began missing as well.

The therapist assured me this was simply another characteristic of RAD. Cain did not trust that anyone would meet his needs so he acted on his own to accomplish them in any way he saw effective. This concept frustrated me. Why couldn't Cain understand we would take care of all his needs? He never wanted for anything materially. He had been in our home for two years now, and he knew we were consistent, nurturing and loving. What more could we possibly do to make him trust us? I tried to remind myself that we were only paying the price for his previous, failed relationship, but it felt personal. Why would he steal from us when there was absolutely nothing we would not give him?

He understood this concept on an intellectual level, but it was obvious he had not internalized it. To add to this frustration was the fact that Cain would not commit to therapy. As the therapist tried to delve into his thoughts, he simply played with the toys in the room and refused to answer questions with anything short of a quick yes or no response. He would ask several times to get a drink of water or use the restroom. I was beginning to feel as if therapy was just Cain's excuse to get out of school.

I would go and pick him up at the school, drive him almost forty minutes to the therapist, wait for an hour while he played with his toys and then drive him the long way back. He had my undivided attention for the entire morning; he controlled it all, and worst of all we were making no progress. The word that best describes a parent of a child that suffers from RAD is frustrated. I could objectively see what Cain would have if he were willing to take the chance to trust, but I could also see it was not within my power to make him take that risk. In addition, the closer I, as a parent, tried to get to Cain, the more he needed to pull away. He perceived closeness as a real threat and further perceived any effort to achieve this closeness as control.

No one could control Cain; he needed each of us in the family to understand this point. He needed teachers and other students to understand this. Whenever he felt a loss of control, his behavior would escalate to regain what he so needed. Control was such an issue because if he gave it up people would certainly hurt him as they had in the past and he needed to control their ability to do that. This thought process obviously created a power struggle. Joe was actually beginning to distance himself from Cain, as had the other children previously. Therefore the real issues, battles and power struggles were between Cain and me.

One particularly frustrating evening came as I was trying to prepare dinner. Cain was sitting at the kitchen table doing his homework with the other children, but his conduct became so distracting that I had to move him. Due to his destructive behavior I could no longer put him in his room alone, so I had him sit down on the hardwood floor in the entrance hall. He had his books, his paper and his pencil, and I told him to finish his homework in there. A few minutes later I came in to check on him. To my dismay, he had used the pencil to carve his name into the hardwood floor.

Frustrated I asked him to move into the living room. Then I finished preparing spaghetti for dinner and asked Amy to take him in his plate. When I went back to the living room I saw that he had taken his entire dinner and smeared it into the white carpet. I was really trying to fight back the tears. I told him to come into the family room where I would be able to see him from the kitchen and to stand there. I had no idea what to do; I tried everything I could think of. I had nowhere I could put Cain so as to find even a few minutes of sanity.

I glanced over at the TV in the family room; a rerun of "Judge Judy" was playing. It was about a woman who worked for a daycare center; when the children were misbehaving, she would make them stand up and hold a can in each hand so they could not get into trouble; I thought this was the craziest thing I had ever heard. Just then I turned my head in time to see a spitball go flying across the island separating the family room from the kitchen and hitting William in the head as he ate his dinner. I looked back at Cain, and he was laughing.

Suddenly I found myself getting two soup cans from the cupboard and handing them to Cain to hold, one in each hand. To my surprise he did this. He stood for a few minutes, but when the other children finished their dinner and returned to the family room Cain made a point to drop the cans. One of them hit the edge of the table and left a huge dent. Cain said he did not mean to do it; his arms just got tired.

I walked into the office, sat down on the sofa and began to cry. I was tired, I was frustrated, and for the first time in my life I wanted to punish a child physically. My parents had disciplined me physically when I was young, and I knew it was not something I ever wanted my child to experience. I was against it, not only because of the emotional scars I believed this form of punishment left, but also because I saw it as ineffective in changing behavior. I felt it served to make a child even angrier and less trustful. Still, I was overwhelmed with this desire to punish him. I had always said I would discipline my children to teach them, but I would never punish them. There was a distinct difference, and yet I wanted to punish Cain. At forty years old, I had never spanked a child and now, it was all I could imagine.

As I sat in that room, sobbing, I wondered what had happened to me; I was really losing it. I had just made my child hold soup cans, I envisioned hurting him, and I felt so alone. I knew Joe was working hard and that we needed him to do that at this time, but I was envious of his ability to leave the house and the problems that existed within. I prayed for guidance and for the welfare of the other children because they too were suffering from my inability to control this situation.

I found myself raising my voice at times to Cain and even saying some hurtful things to him. It was so disturbing; Cain escalated every situation as if his entire goal was to bring me to the point of breaking, and in my own weakness, I was. He seemed to find satisfaction in knocking me off balance and having me doubt myself. I took it all so personally, even though the therapist told me repeatedly not to. I continued to try to show love and compassion to Cain, but it was slowly beginning to feel contrived.

On July 4, a favorite holiday around our house, we invited some friends over to celebrate with us. I had a talk with Cain ahead of time. I thought I had some bargaining power because Cain truly enjoyed fireworks. I pleaded with Cain not to do anything to spoil the evening; in return, he could watch the fireworks.

Recently he had begun vomiting at the table, seemingly at will, in what appeared, at least to me, to be an effort to destroy any kind of family interaction. I begged him not to do that on this night. I should have known that by showing my vulnerability to a certain issue Cain would certainly act on it, and he did. Sure enough, as everyone was eating dinner, he vomited on his plate. Even his love of the fireworks was not enough to allow himself to be controlled.

Joey once showed his vulnerability to Cain with the same outcome. Joey and Colton were on a Little League baseball team. Cain had wanted to join this team for some time but had not made the grades at school or the goals at home to achieve this reward. Still he pushed it, and I decided to address this issue in therapy. The therapist suggested I bring Joey, Colton and Cain in for a session to discuss the possibility. Colton really did not speak; he had endured his share of therapy over the years and was not interested.

Joey did speak, and his words were simple. He told Cain the team meant a lot to him, he was captain, and he had the friendship of his teammates and the respect of his coach. He went on to assure Cain he would be willing for him to join the team and he would make sure the other players accepted him; in return, he wanted only one thing. Joey told Cain he could not handle being embarrassed. "If you promise not to embarrass me with weird behavior or with any of your comments about bodily functions or sexual acts or anything else, I will help you with the team."

Cain was excited and repeatedly promised he would not embarrass Joey. We even went through role-playing at that same session as to how Joey could introduce Cain and what would and would not be appropriate for Cain to say. We played out every possible scenario that might occur and Cain's response to it. By the end of the session Joey felt confident. I think he was proud of himself that he had stepped out of his comfort zone and made a real effort to reach out to Cain.

Baseball season opened only a few days later. All the boys were so excited; the noise and laughter inside the van were deafening as we drove to the field. I was happy too. This was the first normal thing Cain had done in a long time, and I thought it was going to be so good for him. As soon as we reached the field, the kids jumped out of the van and eagerly began catching up with one another. Joey introduced Cain to the rest of the team and then went to the front of the line to begin leading exercise. With that, Cain reached down, grabbed his crotch and yelled, "Let's all try to stretch this." That was the very last time Joey ever reached out to Cain. With each incident, we were all growing further away from Cain, and our hearts were growing harder toward him.

I remember once when Paul ran up the stairs, hollering at me to come quickly. He said someone had done something to his bathroom. The aroma was sickening as I went down the stairs, but nothing prepared me for what I saw when I opened the bathroom door. There was feces spread every-where, on the walls, the shower curtain, the tile, even the linens. Someone had spread toilet tissue all over. Colton said that Cain had gone in there and when he came out it was like that. I asked Cain, and he vehemently denied it, saying it was one of the other kids. He refused to clean it up; he just sat there and defiantly declared he did not do it and would not clean it up. I had no power, he refused, and I had to accept that. I cleaned up the awful mess, and then I did something I will always regret. I spanked him.

That evening I had to go to Denver University. Joey and Colton were attending a football camp there, and this was their first game. Amanda watched the other children while I went. I sat at the field, not believing what I had done. Joey kept asking me if something was wrong, and I kept saying everything was fine. I did not want to take away from his special night. All I could think of was getting back home to tell Cain I was sorry. The guilt I felt was overwhelming. It no longer mattered what Cain had done; the total focus, for me now, was what I had done. That game seemed to last forever; I was sure Cain was home feeling equally awful and that he needed me. A friend came to the game; I wanted to confide in her what I had done, but I was too ashamed. I knew no one who had not experienced living with a child like this could understand. I watched the game in a self-imposed silence and then quickly gathered my things and rushed to the car. Joey and Colton were spending the night at the school; this was good because I was so tired of pretending everything was okay.

It was such a long drive home. I tried to be realistic; I knew I had spanked him with only a few swats with my hand on his jeans, but it wasn't about that; it was about the fact that I had not controlled myself better, that I had let my anger toward him come out in such a manner. I was ashamed of myself. By the time I got home, he was already sleeping. I did not want this to wait until morning, however, so I woke him and told him how sorry I was. He acted as if nothing had happened, as if I had no effect on him whatsoever. He said he did not care; it did not hurt, and I should just forget it.

I thought he could not feel that way and was holding back his true feelings from me so I could not get too close. Regardless of how he really felt, I knew I could not spank him again. What I had done was taken all the responsibility he bore for what he did in the bathroom and placed it on myself for spanking him. It was not effective, and I knew I did not have the heart to do it again. Still, this desire grew with each incident.

More than anything, what happened in the bathroom taught Cain one thing; he did have power. He had power by choosing to control or not control this behavior. He found he had power in urinating on himself if we were on our way somewhere important or urinating around the house on items of his choosing. This passive-aggressive behavior of urinating in any place he chose became his new focus of control. One morning Joey went outside to get the paper from the driveway. He walked back in the front door, and Cain, not knowing he was there, was urinating on the silk tree in the living room.

I pleaded with the therapist for answers. She was a firm believer in natural consequences, as was I. The natural consequence for urinating in inappropriate places was to wear a diaper. She told me to purchase a box of diapers and at first make him wear them at home so as not to embarrass him publicly. She assured me he would most likely change this behavior with the mere threat of having to wear these diapers to school or to sports. I did not like this idea, but I did not have a better one so I agreed.

Unfortunately Cain did not seem to mind. Many times he urinated in the diaper rather than using the bathroom. If I chose to make this into a power struggle, he was sure he would win. He was only eleven, but he had so much power. I remember once we were at a track meet and Cain had a diaper on. As he was running, the diaper began to slip, and the edge of it became noticeable from beneath his shorts. A couple of the kids at the meet made a comment, and I thought for a moment that this would be a turning point.

When Cain came back up the bleachers and sat by me, I asked him if he was embarrassed. He said he was embarrassed only once in his life and that was when his biological mom took him downtown, declaring to the world that Jesus was coming soon. He hid under the flip board she wore. Short of that, nothing was ever going to embarrass him. Even this did not change his behavior; it continued for several more months.

Eventually I grew tired, and since I did know embarrassment and was greatly embarrassed, I told Cain he did not have to wear the diapers anymore. We threw the diapers away, and Cain did not have any further trouble controlling these bodily functions. It was a power struggle; he won, and I lost. He had proven he could endure longer than I could; with that knowledge, he no longer needed to play this game. It was on to the next one.

At about that time a national news story was running about a woman, here in Colorado, accused of killing her young son. She had adopted him and claimed he, too, was suffering from reactive attachment disorder. The prosecution claimed that while her husband was away on business she, in a fit of rage, killed the boy. There was a public outcry that a mother could possess this kind of rage. Her defense attorney did his best to explain what this woman had endured, how alone and unsupported she felt and how she had sought answers from therapists. This was all to no avail; the jury found her guilty and sentenced her to a long term in prison. It seemed everyone felt she got what she deserved. I did not know what she deserved; all I knew was that I had such compassion for her, for her husband, for her poor son and for their struggle. Obviously, what she had done was indefensible—morally, ethically and spiritually wrong—but I felt I could understand how it could have happened; none of us was above that. I wanted to visit her or even just write her, but I was afraid to. I think that if I had contacted her, I would have had to face the reality of my own feelings of anger and growing rage.

Shortly after this case, another one came to the forefront. This one was also local and involved another adopted child suffering from RAD. The parents, at their breaking point, brought their child to a clinic in Evergreen. One theory in the treatment of RAD is rebirthing. It is a procedure wherein the therapist creates a scenario that simulates the birth of the child. In this particular case they wrapped the child in a blanket; the adults surrounded the child and held the blanket tight, with strong pressure to represent the womb. The child was then to struggle as in childbirth to free herself from this artificial womb, only this time into the arms of her adopted mother, thus initiating an attachment with her. This philosophy has its share of critics, me being one, but it also has its share of supporters.

Sadly this procedure went very wrong. The young struggling girl tried desperately to convey her inability to breath, but the therapists involved believed she either was acting defiantly or was not in a life-threatening situation; they were wrong. She died that afternoon of asphyxiation. The therapist and the adopted mom were charged with the death. Again a mother was charged in the death of her adopted child suffering from RAD.

My only hope from this case as well as the other was to bring public attention to this disorder and to the lack of support and education available to the families of these children. Regrettably, as quickly as these stories gained public interest and notoriety they faded into the background. People, who for a moment tried to understand the despair, had now turned their thoughts onto the next story. Again the families of this terrible disorder suffered alone.

The majority of the pain a child with RAD feels and then tries to inflict upon others is directed at the mother. She is the most threatening because she possesses control within the family and because she seeks intimacy; this was true in our case as well. All the kids by now had 'checked out' in their ability or willingness to acknowledge this situation. Joe, by his own admission, had given up on the situation. I felt a degree of resentment because I was the only one who did not have that option.

I still needed to deal with the therapists, the school and the destructive behaviors he exhibited at home. I felt a sense of hopelessness and knew I was sinking into a deeper and darker place each day. I could only imagine the judgment of others. Cain was truly ill, and yet I was angry with him for a sickness he perhaps could not control. I placed that same judgment on myself, only adding to my despair. I found that at his therapy sessions I was doing most of the talking. Unconsciously I guess I decided if he was making no use of these sessions, I would. The therapist told me I was too involved. I needed to let go of him and see him as nothing more than a boarder in our home. She reiterated that he was not and could not ever be an active member of any family; what I was asking of him was impossible.

I heard those words, but I had no idea how to accomplish such a feat. What was I supposed to do? Was I supposed to ignore all his behaviors, hold him to a different standard than the rest of the children? How could I discipline them for a particular behavior and then allow Cain to bear no consequence for the same behavior? He was not a boarder; he was my responsibility, legally and morally. I would still be the one the school called, the one the other children ran to when Cain did something bizarre. What she was asking of me was impossible.

I asked her to explain to me, step by step, what I should do. She told me to take everything from his room including his clothes and move all of it out, leaving only the mattress. He could have the clothes he had on, but everything else he would have to earn. Then I was to leave him to lie on the bed day after day until he decided to accept the rules. I knew there was no possibility of this working. Cain would not put forward the effort to gain anything. This would turn out to be another power struggle, like the diapers.

Even if I had believed this had the slightest possibility of working, I did not know if I had the stomach for it. She assured me he would be treated even worse than this if he were placed in a hospital, which was where he was heading if his behavior worsened. Nevertheless, our home was not a hospital, and we had given up so much of our family already to this illness, that to have to deal with this new request, on a daily basis, was more than I could personally handle. I did not have the luxury of changing shifts each eight hours like those at the hospital. It was only me, twenty-four hours a day, every day, and I was just so tired.

Sleep had become a luxury. We discovered Cain was getting up in the middle of the night and roaming the house. He later told me he used this time to do things deliberately to make me think I was going crazy. He hid papers I needed, took checks, threw important documents away and made it a game to see what he could do that would have the greatest effect on me. I, of course, having no knowledge of this plan, believed the stress was causing me to lose my mind.

Cain's behavior, although odd and certainly weird was, at least, nonviolent. I had heard horror stories from other parents of children like Cain involving acts of violence against their families. I was thankful that was not an issue for us — that is, until the day I happened upon Cain's spelling list. It was ordinary — just a list of words the teacher had given him. I looked down the list, and then my heart actually skipped a beat. His spelling word was *revenge,* and next to it was written the word *family.* I asked Cain about it, and, as in the past, he simply said he did not do it. Someone else must have taken his paper and written this on it. I did not believe what he said; the only thing I believed for sure was that the days of nonviolence were over.

About this time I started smelling what I thought to be smoke in the house. Joe and the other children smelled it as well. We searched every bit of the house and could not find anything; yet the smell of something burning was strong. This smell was not all the time; sporadically it appeared and then disappeared. Each time our anxiety grew since we had no idea what was going on. It was several weeks before we discovered Cain was lighting paper in his room and dropping it down the heat vent causing the smell to emanate from seemingly everywhere. When Joe asked Cain why he would do such a thing, Cain's response was that he thought it was funny to see us run around and try to figure out what was burning. From that point on we kept the lighter we had used for candles locked in the safe. We knew this was not an answer; we had a gas stove so Cain could get fire if he wanted to. Still, it was something we could do, and there was so little left we could. We learned from the therapist that an obsession with fire is true of many children with RAD.

The next cause of concern came in a paper that Cain had either unintentionally dropped on the garage floor as he was leaving for school or intentionally dropped in an effort to let us know exactly what he was thinking. The note was titled "How to Kill My Family." A number of options were listed, including knife, gun, rat poison and so on. The rat poison was circled and identified by the marking "best option." I read those words and then hesitantly looked for the rat poison I knew we kept on the shelf, afraid it was not there; to my relief it was. I grabbed the poison, but I did not know what to do with it. I didn't think I should put it down the drain. I did not want to put it in the trash because I was sure Cain would pull it back out again. Finally I decided to wrap it up in one bag after another then take it to the dumpster by the club-house. I had taken his poison away for the day; but I knew if he really wanted to kill us, there would always be a way.

It is impossible to convey the depths of our anguish and our hopelessness. We had no semblance of family life anymore. We lived with a very ill child, and his illness penetrated each of us. It was as if his behaviors were causing us to behave differently. We had never had anger or rage in our home, and his anger and rage against us sliced into a part of our psyche we did not even know existed. I was not an angry person. I was, if anything, overly optimistic. I considered myself kind, gentle and loving in nature.

Yet there was one night that showed me I too had a dark side. Cain did not come home for dinner. It was getting dark outside and was raining. I got in the car to drive around the neighborhood to look for him. I should have been home with my husband and children enjoying a family dinner; instead I was driving around in a rainstorm, looking for Cain.

I could sense my anger was building. I began to replay the past months in my mind, each memory intensifying the resentment and fury. I could not live in fear anymore, and I could not allow my family to live in this insanity anymore; we were losing ourselves to this madness. In the headlights, through the sweep of the windshield wiper and my tears, I saw Cain. He was just standing there in the rain oblivious to the fact that I was there. I was sure his sole purpose in being there was to add to the insanity. The thought of pressing my foot to the gas and running into him overwhelmed me. I could say it was an accident and the car had slid in the rain. He did not even know I was there. No one would believe a mother could do such a thing on purpose. I wanted to step on the gas; there was no denying that. Only divine intervention made me finally move my foot from above the gas pedal back onto the brake and instead to roll down the window and call him over. He had pushed me to a place I had never been before, a place of total surrender and total defeat.

A few days later Cain and I were having an in-depth talk. He was more vulnerable than he had been in a while, and I felt he was being as honest with me as he could about what he felt. He said a recurring dream haunted him. In the dream his biological father and he would kill every member of our family with a knife. He went on to say that in the dream he repeatedly saw our dead bodies lying on the family room floor. He saw blood everywhere, but he had no ability to stop it. It was not his fault. Still he was saddened by it. He drew a picture of this dream, on my request, and the details made me nauseous.

I wondered if Cain really wanted to hurt us or simply wanted us to believe he would because it gave him power in our home. I still believed Cain felt some form of love for us and in the end would not want us dead or injured. Undeniably his actions did not support this premise. My degree of concern was ever increasing. One night, after we returned from church, I went up to Cain's room to tuck him in. Joe was with me. As I kissed him goodnight, I noticed a long slash in his mattress running half the length of the bed. Inside this slash was the butcher knife from the kitchen. Cain swore he did not make the slash nor did he insert the knife; someone again was trying to set him up.

This grabbed even Joe's attention; he now saw the seriousness of the situation. His involvement and concern, however, were not as comforting as I had imagined. It only made me more concerned; if he thought it was serious, it must be serious. I had resented Joe for a long time for not being more "plugged in," but what I was beginning to realize was that he was the only normalcy the other children knew through this traumatic time. He still took them bowling, hiking, to the movies—all the things we could not do with Cain. If he had been in the same place as I was, the children would have been drawn through the middle of this. He was their refuge, but now he could no longer wait with them on the sideline. He knew we had to do something.

Joe and Joey had a golf trip planned for the following weekend. Joe wanted to cancel it, but I knew Joey had been looking forward to this time away with his dad. They had already given up so much to Cain's illness. I wanted them both to have this trip. It was only to the mountains, and they would be back in a few days. I finally persuaded them to go. No sooner had they left on Friday morning than I realized it was a terrible mistake. Cain's behavior deteriorated rapidly. Maybe it was Joe not being there, or maybe the illness was just progressing—but for the very first time I was truly afraid of Cain.

By late afternoon Cain had sealed our fate. He came to me in the family room, sat down quietly next to me and looked at me with great sadness. He then said, "I don't want to hurt you, but I think I will. You better sleep with your door locked tonight."

I had to catch my breath and take a moment before I could reply. "Do you really think you will hurt me?"

With that, he put his head down and nodded yes. I could not think. Joe was a few hours away, and it was late Friday afternoon. I did not know what to do. I told Cain to go to his room and wait for me; he did. I then started calling anyone I could think of. First I called Social Services. Cain did not have a current case open so they were sorry but they could do nothing at this time. I could file a report, and someone would get back with me to investigate the situation; but they were not able to provide crisis intervention for something like this. I knew the likelihood of their "promptly" calling me back was slim. They are definitely there for you before the adoption, but it is not as easy to get them to return a phone call after the adoption if you don't have an open case. I then called the mental health facility we had been using. Cain's therapist had left for the weekend, and I was told they too did not provide this type of crisis intervention. Our therapist could refer him, if she deemed it necessary, to another doctor, but that could not take place until Monday.

Then, for some reason and I do not recall why, I turned in the phone book to the listing for attorneys. Maybe I thought I could somehow force Social Services into intervening on our behalf, even though I knew how long that would take. Still I turned the pages. I looked under family law, adoptions and so forth when a little ad caught my eye. It said, "How to get him out and keep him out." I called the number not knowing what to expect. To my surprise the attorney answered the phone. By now it was almost 5:00. She asked me what was going on, and as I began to tell her the tears started flowing. Briefly I told her of the last two years of our lives and how we had lost our family to this illness. I feared not only for us in what Cain might do, but also for him. He needed help I could not provide.

It was odd because she listened so intently. She was nothing I expected from a stranger. She asked one question after another and seemed more concerned than even the therapists we had been seeing. She was compassionate and empathetic. I wondered if at some point in her life she had dealt with a similar situation. She actually tried to comfort me, never once speaking about a retainer or coming into her office. She said, "Let me see what I can do. Stay strong and stay safe until we can get you help." I looked at the clock and realized she had been speaking with me for almost forty-five minutes. I felt calmed by talking with her. I knew that at least someone else now knew what was going on in our home.

When the violence first started, Joe and I began keeping notes and other items relating to the threats Cain was making in the safe, along with a letter that if we were ever murdered Cain had done it. The file we created contained not just the papers I had found, but the picture he had drawn of all of us murdered, as well as the lighters and knives we had taken from his room. It was all there. Even so, there was no comfort in that, but now a real person knew. Whatever would happen that weekend, someone would know what we were going through. She would be a witness to any pending tragedy; I found this empowering. What would happen would happen— I could not control that—but the truth would come out.

I took a few minutes to pray about this and to give it some serious consideration. Through this prayer I realized, based on experience, Cain was able to control his behavior if he wanted to. Now, in a more rational state, I could see the comments he had made earlier may have been in an effort to manipulate me. Even if they were not, he had warned me of his intentions, and to me that meant, at least to some degree, he did not want to hurt me. The truth was if he wanted to hurt me, he would; but I still wanted to believe he did not. I needed to show him I still cared about him and believed deep down he cared about me.

I told Cain to come up from his room, and I told him how much I loved him and how sad I was to see him in pain and that I appreciated the fact that he was trying to be honest with me. Then I told him I had reported all of his behavior to the authorities and that there was now a record of what he was planning to do. I told him about the items I had in the safe and assured him that even if he killed me, Joe would turn those items over to the police and everyone would know what he had done.

I could not tell if he believed me or not; he made no indication either way. He was angry—that was obvious. That night he slept in his room. Well, he went to bed in his room; I have no idea what he really did. The other kids slept on the floor in my bedroom behind a locked door. I stayed with them, awake each night, to keep watch. I heard noises through the night but decided it was not worth a confrontation. Whatever Cain did to the house we would just have to deal with. More important, I had to keep everyone safe.

Cain and I did not speak the rest of the weekend. He was angry with me, and I did not want to escalate the situation; we coexisted for the longest weekend of both of our lives.

Joe returned Sunday afternoon and, in anguish of learning the details of the weekend, decided this had to end. We had nothing more to offer, and the negative impact of Cain's presence had become unbearable. We had no idea what the next move was, but we did know we needed to make one. We could no longer let our family suffer in this silence and the refusal of therapists or Social Services to intervene. Monday morning brought some answers.

Early in the day I received a phone call from the mental health crisis center. The caller said an attorney, acting on our behalf, had requested an emergency psychiatric evaluation for Cain. The woman I had called on Friday afternoon had not forgotten us; she had advocated on our behalf, and now we had the opportunity we sought. We needed to have Cain there within the hour.

Joey and Amanda decided to come with us, maybe because they sensed my fragility or maybe because they too would be affected by the imminent outcome of this psych exam. We brought the items from the safe. I was afraid that once we were there Cain would present normal, as he could if he wanted to, and they would send us back home.

Joe and I went back to the exam room with Cain. The doctor looked at the picture of us dead and asked Cain if we were safe. To our surprise Cain told the truth when he answered, "I think I might hurt them." There was no more talk. The doctor looked at us and informed us Cain was going to the hospital for a minimum of three days to be completely evaluated. Our only decision was whether we wanted him taken by ambulance or if we wanted to drive him. Cain looked to us, and I knew we had come this far together; we would take him. The doctor told us not to go home to retrieve his belongings, but instead to go straight to the hospital. He signed the papers, and as quickly as he had appeared he was gone. We had been there less than fifteen minutes. The receptionist gave us directions, and in silence we walked down the stairs.

It was close to lunch, and we were afraid Cain would not arrive in time to eat so we stopped for fast food on the way. Cain barely ate a thing. I could not imagine what he was going through. I sensed his fear, and I think he sensed mine. All of us were quiet for the rest of the trip. The only question Cain asked was if we were sure it was only three days. We reiterated what we had been told earlier.

We rang the bell and waited for the orderly to come to the entrance. The building was old; it had the usual hospital smell and the sounds of what appeared to be some very disturbed people. We then walked past an isolation room into a main area. The orderly told Cain to sit at the table, and he would be right back with the nurse. He told us we would need to leave then. I asked if we could stay and talk with the nurse; he quickly interrupted and said he needed to walk us out. Cain stood, and we each in turn walked over and gave him a hug. I told him I loved him, and he told me he loved me too. Joey and Amanda said their good-byes, and then Joe gave him a hug. By this time Cain's tears were beginning to flow. I looked back at him one last time as we headed toward the door; he was crying. I had not seen him cry in such a long time. I did not want to leave him there, but I knew he could not come back home with us. The doctor had assured us this was only a three-day visit, but even three days were enough. I just needed to rest.

We could not have known then that Cain would never again live in our home.

An excerpt from "The Prophet" by Kahlil Gibran

*And a woman who held a babe against her bosom
said, "Speak to us of Children".
And he said:*

*Your children are not your children,
They are the sons and daughters of
Life's longing for itself.
They come through you but are not from you,
And though they are with you
yet they belong not to you.*

*You may give them your love but not your thoughts,
For they have their own thoughts.
You may house their bodies but not their souls,
For their souls dwell in the house of tomorrow,
which you cannot visit, not even in your dreams.
You may strive to be like them, but seek
not to make them like you.
For life goes not backward
nor tarries with yesterday.*

*You are the bows from which your children
as living arrows are sent forth.
The archer sees the mark upon
the path of the infinite, and
He bends you with His might that
His arrows may go swift and far.
Let your bending in the archer's hand
be for gladness;*

*For even as He loves the arrow that flies,
So he loves also the bow that is stable.*

Chapter Six

Doubt

As I continued the hard work of restoring this once beautiful verandah, I thought back on that little bunny. I, unlike the bunny, had survived, but maybe I had been wrong about that being enough. Was simply surviving all that mattered, or was there instead another factor I was not considering? If that bunny had survived but wounded in some way, could it have then fended off the next adversity to affect it? I had survived, but I had been so severely wounded by my loss of confidence that I wondered if I too could fend off the next adversity. This gave me even more reason to continue with the process of remembering.

Doubt had now set into our ministry. We had once believed we were going to change the world. We could not; we could not even change the lives of these children. It was a realization of extreme powerlessness; still it was more than that. I had defined myself as a mother. I had lost all other titles in my life, and I was fine with that. I loved being a mother, and as a bonus I once believed I was good at it. I had dreamt of taking in more children and sharing the love of our family with all those who needed it. And now I did not even have the confidence to parent the ones I still had.

We had lost Shin, Shelby, Benjamin and now Cain. I had thought that if I truly loved a child, comforted them, nurtured them and made them feel like the most special child in the world that my love would heal them. Our love as a family would heal them. I still struggle with the idea that there are times when love is not enough.

I did not know how it would be possible to continue taking children into our home when the truth was, I had no idea what they truly needed. I knew how to parent emotionally healthy children; I did not know how to parent children who had suffered in the ways these children had. I had no training, no support and no idea where to go from here.

I had not been able to save Shin. We later heard she had in fact joined a gang and was living in a group home until she ran away again. Our doctor told us Shin had been in for a pregnancy test although she could not disclose the results. I found that news so disturbing because Shin had not healed from the wounds of her childhood, and yet she was now going to be the parent.

Further I had not been able to save Cain. My love was not enough to overcome those early years. He was hospitalized, and all I had managed to do was inflict more pain on our family by trying too long to prove to myself I could make a difference. That is probably my greatest regret. I do not regret Cain's coming to live with us or even the early years, but the last two years of his time here were partially my fault. I was unwilling to see the truth, and in some ways I was parenting from a sense of guilt. To this day I am not sure where that guilt originated, but I carried it. Maybe it was because I knew how different the younger years of these children's lives were from my own children. My own children had wanted for nothing, and these children had wanted for everything. The problem is my biological children suffered in the loss of part of their childhood because of this skewed thought process.

Last, I had not been able to keep Shelby and Benjamin. My heart continued to break for their loss. Joe tried to comfort me by reminding me of our original goal. We wanted to take in children no one else wanted. Another family wanted Shelby and Benjamin, and so if we were to abide by that original philosophy we needed to let them go. I agreed, but that in no way compensated for the incredible sense of loss and grief.

I became depressed. I once felt I had purpose for my life; now I could see none. When Joe and I were first married I did not intend to have children. My goal was law school and then some great career. He wanted a big family. He was so enthusiastic I somehow caught his excitement. I wondered if that had been a mistake, if I should have taken a different road with my life—one I had the opportunity to be more successful on. I had trouble seeing that Amanda, Joey, Amy, Paul, Colton, Marissa, William and Johnny still needed me.

It was at this time Amy reminded me of a quote by Gandhi: "Be the change you want to see in the world." I had not changed the world, but I had let it change me. I was not the innocent, overly optimistic, young-at-heart girl I had been before all this happened. I needed to find a way back to me, and to do so I would need to let go of my futile view of the world, let go of my pessimism and my cynicism and become the woman God had envisioned, not the one who had lost herself amidst failure.

I continued to drive out to the hospital to see Cain each week and participate in his therapy. I found myself looking forward to this time as if it were my own therapy. I monopolized much of the time seeking my own answers to life. This worked out well. Cain wanted nothing to do with therapy, and I wanted everything to do with it, so we shared.

I struggled with guilt; Cain never had any. I struggled with self-doubt; Cain only doubted others. I feared more failure; Cain risked nothing so he had nothing to lose. We were quite a pair as we continued with this ritual for almost a year.

I made some progress. By finally accepting the reality that God changes the lives of those He touches, not me, I had to accept that I was not responsible for each choice of each individual. I had not healed Cain, but I had not made him sick either. I had given him the opportunity to make other choices, supported by my love and our family's love, but he was responsible for those choices.

The same went for Shin. I let go of the guilt because I had not abused her or even been the one to abandon her in a foreign country. I had only sought to heal those existing wounds; our whole family had.

By making some progress—I mean I was able to say those words—accepting them had not yet happened. I knew in my mind that what happened with both of them was not my fault, but I could not yet acknowledge that in my heart.

Cain deteriorated. He was eventually transferred to a residential treatment center and then another and another and finally another. He did not find success in any of them. But our relationship with him did improve over time. I learned I should not reach out to him but instead let him reach toward us. I never call him; he calls when he wants to speak with us, and we are always there for him. He needs to feel in control—that I learned. As he has grown older he has been given passes to come back to the house for a day or two to visit. I am never sure if he really enjoys that time or if he just wants to stay connected. Cain never really wanted a family—well, not the responsibilities and attachments that come from one. I have always said he would have been happy with only a picture of our family on the wall. He would have the assurance he would never be alone and would have a family to show others—because even though he never wanted a family, he was fully aware that other people did. Sometimes, through his sadness, I sensed he wished he could want it as well.

We had the choice to terminate parental rights. It would have been so much easier, but instead we hired an attorney and went to court against Social Services. It was our belief that everyone else in Cain's life had abandoned him; we could not be just one more. We had to stick it out, no matter what it cost, financially and emotionally.

The judge ruled in our favor, and our parental rights were kept intact. But this decision later allowed the state to seek child support from us since Cain was our child and no longer lived in our home. We continue to visit him, attend therapy and make ourselves available to him.

In the end Cain made some very bad decisions, yet he made a few good ones as well. He graduated from high school, was able to emancipate from Social Services and was accepted into college. Cain wanted these things, enough to work for them, because they benefited him. If only he could someday see this same value in people and in relationships.

We had survived these years of doubt. I accepted that my role as mother was imperfect, flawed, and flourished only under God's grace. We grew so much during these years, and the doubt as to who we were was resolved. We realized we were nothing more than the children of God, incapable of changing the world, our only objective remaining that it not change us.

Chapter Seven

The Risk in Friendship

Back on the verandah I was beginning to see some real progress. I looked to the flowers that were subtly beginning to blossom. I was intrigued by how earlier in the morning they were reaching toward the east, trying to find the sun, one flower leaning on the other in an effort to find what it needed to survive. Afterward, at least for a while, they stood straight up, needing no support, instead directly finding their own sun. Only hours later the flowers that had been so strong were now being held down by the flowers reaching over them, in their attempt to follow the sun. It made me think of how there are times in our lives when we stand strong, other times when we are supported by those around us and, finally, times when we are simply there for those around us to lean on.

My best friend, Monet, was witness to our life as we were to hers. She had seen the struggles we had endured as a family, but she had also seen the times when the children made great progress and we found immense joy. We were at a happy and peaceful place in our lives, and she, like everyone else, could sense it. There had been a price to pay to get here, but that cost certainly did not outweigh the incredible reward.

One night Social Services asked us to take a young African-American girl named Shaniqua for a few days while they found her a placement. Since Monet too is black, I went to her to ask about how to care for Shaniqua's hair. Monet helped, and while doing so we had a chance to talk. She and her husband had two boys, but she had always wanted a daughter as well. She had been open to the idea of adopting for some time. Convincing her husband, Damon, was another feat, but nothing was impossible for Monet.

Like us, Monet and Damon were asked to visit with children for prospective placement. They met a young girl who was in the custody of Social Services after her adoptive placement failed and the adoptive parents returned her to the system. Her problems became evident after several visitations, and Monet and Damon decided they would continue visiting with other children. They met several young girls, each having some rather serious problems.

Finally they came upon a beautiful newborn girl. They were very interested, but as in most placements she had a sibling, a two-and-a-half-year-old sister. Monet and Damon, like us, had no intention of taking in more than one child; now they too were faced with an enormous decision. They were concerned because the baby, Olivia, was born cocaine addicted. It was not known if the older girl, Venus, had been as well. Both girls shared the same mother who was a prostitute, but the dad was unknown for both. There was not much family history on either.

Monet and Damon decided to take the girls for several overnight visits and through much prayer and contemplation made the difficult choice to take in both girls. The decision was made more difficult by the seriousness of the situation the girls were taken from; in all likelihood they were not a short-term placement. The courts would pursue termination of parental rights, and the girls would be eligible for adoption; this was a serious commitment.

Venus presented with some oppositional behavior; but so do most two year olds, and nothing was deemed out of the ordinary. Olivia presented as any newborn and, through much love and nurturing by Monet, could not have been a happier baby, suffering only minor effects from the early drug addiction. The decision seemed to be the right one, and Monet and Damon certainly had the ability and desire to give both girls every possible opportunity. Their other two boys accepted the girls without hesitation, and in no time at all they became a family.

Despite their joy there was also the incredible stress a decision like this can put on a marriage and a family. With pregnancy there is a period of adjustment and anticipation; with adoption there is not. With adoption there is suddenly another or even more than one other child with his or her own needs, hurts and demands on time. This stress was not oblivious to either Monet or Damon.

This was exacerbated by the fact that Venus was becoming more and more difficult. Shortly after the adoption she was diagnosed with reactive attachment disorder, oppositional defiance disorder and post-traumatic stress disorder. She attended regular therapy and within time was placed into therapeutic preschool and then kindergarten. As with Cain, and most children who suffer from RAD, the mother is the enemy. There exists a great desire within the child to separate the mother and father and then to ally with the father; this is precisely what happened. Venus was conscious of her behavior when Damon was present and was able to remain calm. When alone with Monet, she would scream and yell, throw tantrums, demand her way, be secretive, destructive and manipulative. This caused each parent to see a very different child and was instrumental in causing division.

Eventually the stress became too great, and Monet and Damon made the decision to separate. Monet, once a married mother of two children, had, within a short time, become the single mother of four children, one of whom was becoming increasingly ill. It was also difficult for us since we felt some responsibility for Monet's decision to take the girls. Still no one could argue that Olivia was thriving and becoming such an exceptional young girl that it would have been so incredibly wrong for Monet not to have taken her in.

Nevertheless, each day offered a new array of problems. Monet was working full time and had placed the girls in a daycare center. Unfortunately, because of Venus's uncontrollable behavior, the girls were asked to leave, and Venus was not allowed to return. After this, finding daycare was almost impossible. Monet worked for a small company, and her employer, sensing her desperation, allowed her to bring the girls to work with her. Trying to work full time, make necessary phone calls and complete the day's work was trying enough, but with two small children to care for at the same time it became more than most could bear. Venus was able to pick up on this and realized she possessed a great deal of power. By simply screaming at the top of her lungs, or acting out when Monet was on the phone, she could get what she wanted.

Monet realized the seriousness of the situation and as such contacted the county department to obtain help. Prior to the adoption, Social Services had made it clear they would be supportive of the family after the adoption was finalized, but that was not the case. Monet sought respite care; this is a service offered by and paid for by Social Services to provide rest for stressed parents who desperately need a break. The child is placed in an alternative foster home until the situation decompresses and both the child and the parent have had a little time apart. It is a good program. When Monet called, however, she was told the program was available only to foster parents; it was not available to parents once the adoption was finalized. Social Services then offered no alternatives, no suggestions and no answers for an impossible situation.

A short time later Monet was at a crucial point at work when Venus began screaming. Monet tried the usual routine of putting her in another room with crayons and a coloring book and giving her a snack. She then tried talking with her in a rational manner, which had proved futile prior to this day, and remained so. Finally, in a moment of desperation, she took Venus out to the car and put her in it with the window rolled part way down. Venus continued to scream; Monet could see her from inside the office. She watched for a few minutes and then, when she realized Venus was going to continue to scream, decided to get in at least a few minutes of work before she brought her back in. Altogether Venus was in the car for about ten minutes when the police arrived at Monet's office. Apparently a woman from a few doors down had seen what happened and had called the police. Monet was interrogated as was Venus, and then Monet was charged with child neglect.

Within days her case was turned over to Social Services. Monet was contacted with the news that a caseworker was at the elementary school questioning her children as to whether they had been abused or not. Her oldest son felt that he was pressured to say something derogatory about his mother, but he refused to because he was truthful. Monet appeared before Social Services to defend her actions in a continued investigation. Unfortunately, by all accounts a decision had already been made. The allegation was deemed founded, a case was opened, and Monet was referred to the National Child Abuse Registry.

It was only at this time that Social Services took any interest in what was going on. Sadly, the system is reactive not proactive. What happened was wrong—there is no denying that fact—but it was foreseeable and preventable. If Monet had not made the unselfish decision to adopt these girls and instead kept them as foster children, she would have been entitled to help. Because she had adopted them and as such was not eligible for any county crisis intervention, she now faced criminal charges, the potential loss of her other children, legal costs, probation and loss of reputation.

Some good did come from this, however. A caseworker was assigned to the family, and the incredible needs of Venus were revealed. Through some therapeutic intervention it was determined that Venus needed a greater degree of care. A meeting was called, and it was decided that she would be placed in Denver Christian Home. This placement has a good reputation, but even they were not able to help Venus. It was a therapist at this location who determined further therapy with Venus would prove unsuccessful. She was unengaged; she slept through appointments, manipulated others and let everyone know she did not intend to play this game. The therapist decided Venus was not utilizing this placement as well as another needy child could, and so Venus was moved to a foster home.

Monet still committed to therapy with Venus and to weekend visitations although it was becoming more and more evident to everyone that Venus was gaining no benefit from a family situation. She did not thrive at the foster home, but she did as well there as she did anywhere. In some ways she may even have done better because she was just one of many. There were no expectations of her, no pressure of intimacy or family closeness. It was a bit of healing time for Monet and the other children.

Just when the situation was getting a little better, Monet was notified by Social Services that, because of a major funding shortage, Venus would be returned home. No one believed it was in the best interest of Monet and the other children; but, according to the county, there were no other options. So a child, who had learned more in her time away about the system and more about manipulation and control, was returned to a family that was just beginning to find a peace it had been missing for so long.

What happened next was expected; Venus returned but separated herself from the family. Her behavior so paralleled Cain's. Monet suffered a gamut of false allegations, reports from the school and even moments of great despair.

Like me, she studied reactive attachment disorder. She did this to understand Venus and, by doing so, be better able to meet her needs. Unfortunately understanding is not enough with this disorder. Venus deteriorated over the years, and as her sister, Olivia, flourished Venus sank deeper and deeper into a world she created and only she understood.

Olivia's success was only an added stress for Venus. She knew either she could not function on that same level or she was not willing to put the effort into it to get there. Either way her resentment turned toward her sister on several occasions. The most notable was in a swimming pool where Venus climbed on her sister's back and held her under the water. From that point on, the girls could not be left alone together for fear Venus would harm Olivia.

Monet struggled with questions to which there are no answers. Venus is still young; the future is so uncertain. The only certainty is that the early years of her life affected her so dramatically that she will, in all likelihood, never be able to attach to anyone.

In an odd way Monet's story and her experiences with Venus helped us to heal because we could see the illness was part of the child. We could be objective with Venus because we were not so invested. Objectively we saw nothing could be done that Monet was not already doing.

I am saddened that God has allowed my friend to share the same pain we endured. I am thankful, though, that we had each other, because we understood something no one else could ever understand. We both came to know an inconceivable inner despair; one that brought us to places we never knew existed within our minds. More than that, we both learned how to face that unspeakable anguish, like so many other parents of children diagnosed with RAD, with so little support.

Despite that, Monet successfully finished the probation she had been sentenced to, and her name was removed from the National Registry. She went back to school and completed her paramedic training; this allows her to work two jobs to support her family. She maintained custody of all four of her children throughout the investigation and any other claims of abuse against her were declared unfounded. She continues to show great strength of character in parenting a child with RAD.

Chapter Eight

The Happy Years

As I stood up from my rocking chair, I looked over to my once blooming rose garden, now withered and dead. I was startled to notice that although the roses had long since perished, leaving behind only brittle stalks sprouting crisp brown leaves, the bottoms of the bushes were once again beginning to turn green. The dead foliage was being pushed further and further away from the new life. Despite the severity of what they had endured, they continued to grow and with this growth negated the harshness of the past years.

I felt a peace moving into our lives; we all did. We had suffered, but as with any storm when it passes, there is an undeniable peace. We were able to look back at Shelby and Benjamin with fond memories, instead of hurt. We looked back at Shin and saw the wounded child we knew, and we prayed for the young woman God knew. We made our peace with Cain and even began to enjoy his company on family visits.

The business was beginning to show growth. As in most new businesses, especially construction, it had struggled financially in the beginning and required so much of Joe's time and resources. However, even in those lean times, Joe still made sure no one did without; he was accomplished in the art of bartering. He even arranged to work as the General Contractor on the home of our Orthodontist in return for braces for the children. Eight out of the nine needed them so it was certainly a concern. We were also blessed with wonderful organizations like the Schmitz Family Foundation and the Ace Scholarship Program that helped us in sending the children to private school. We were fortunate in wanting for nothing that God did not provide for us.

We understood the lessons we had been taught and were thankful for the opportunities we had been given. We decided not to take in any more children and even let our license lapse so we would not be tempted. We decided instead to love and adore our nine children. People sensed our happiness. We were "The Brady Bunch."

We were very involved in our church. We attended weekly as a family, and the kids attended a youth ministry during the week. They loved the youth pastor, Navin, and his assistant. They led the kids on two separate mission trips, one to Arkansas and the other to St. Louis.

We were happy that the children felt so at home at this Church. I had been raised Catholic, even through University; Joe converted to Catholicism before our wedding. Each of our biological children were baptized in the same Catholic Church in which Joe and I were married and at which we attended until the first foster children came to live with us. It was at this time that we were encouraged to consider a non-denominational church that would meet the varying needs of our many children. In doing so, we could show them all the options and then let them chose for themselves. We were reluctant at first but we knew the needs of all superseded the needs of any one so we began looking for a new church home. It was my friend Monet that first asked us to attend this church.

One afternoon, while I was waiting for Paul and Willy to finish school, the thought struck me that the church had so many activities for the high-school children, but activities were limited for the middle-school kids. I had the idea of creating an after-school program at the church and inviting the junior-high students from the neighboring five schools.

I thought it would be fun if we had open basketball courts, crafts, ping-pong and games. I thought we could have loud Christian music playing and offer concessions, but most of all we could just be there for the kids. I thought all these things, but the truth is that Joe thought of them years earlier. He used to drive through downtown Denver and look at old buildings dreaming of converting them into gyms for under-privileged children. He always had a heart for this, and it was his enthusiasm that encouraged me to continue.

I did a little research and discovered the hours directly after school and before Mom or Dad got home from work were the most dangerous hours of the day for a child. The temptation during these unsupervised times often won over. I contacted several schools and found much support, so I brought the idea to our pastor, Thomas.

Pastor Thomas said, "Put something in writing and get it to the junior-high pastor, and we will see where it goes."

I did just that. I wrote a proposal with Joe's help and had it submitted within the week. To my surprise, only a few days later the youth pastor contacted me to arrange a meeting. From that moment on things happened quickly, and before I knew it Joe and I were printing flyers, arranging for volun-teers, buying concessions and planning for our after-school program. The first day of the program was set for September 11, 2001. The tragedies of that day forced us to cancel the very first program.

The next weeks went smoother. Before we knew it we had twenty kids, then forty, then sixty and even some weeks a hundred. We began to have some trouble arranging for transportation. Joe always made sure he was off work in time to go and pick up the kids. We had been using several vans, including our big blue fifteen-passenger van as well as some of those belonging to the other volunteers. But it was becoming increasingly evident that we needed a bus, a great big old school bus. That became my dream.

I started writing letters to local businesses asking for support, and no one was more surprised than I when they responded positively. We were starting to raise the money, but we still had the problem of where to find an old school bus. Then, just as everything else had fallen into place, a woman I had met only a few times at the church approached me with where we could get our bus. Navin went out to see it that week, and before long our big yellow bus sat behind the church waiting for school to start up again.

We were blessed with incredible volunteers who came every week. Theresa had a gift for crafts and was creative and a great role model. Joe ran the open basketball in the gym, which was partly about basketball and a lot about mentoring. The young boys started looking up to him, and he was always willing to reach out a little further and draw them in. Monet often helped Joe and, because of her own sons, had great interaction with the middle-school boys. Friends of ours who did not attend the church volunteered as well. They were the proof that this was not about our church; it was about our community, and we could all come together for the good of the children.

By the second year we began a secondary ministry offering volunteer leadership positions to high-school students so they could mentor the junior-high kids. We were learning some of the mistakes we had made and were doing a good job of accommodating ever-changing needs. Each of us began developing personal relationships with the kids who attended. They told us of their problems, and sometimes we offered advice; most of the time we just listened. We hugged them, laughed with them and sometimes cried with them, but we always did our best to make them feel loved. In doing so, we were the ones who felt love.

Despite its many positive attributes, this program was not without controversy. The kids sometimes went a little wild; this was difficult because it was, after all, still a church setting. There were issues with boys and girls trying to sneak off together for stolen moments and water fights in the bathroom. Some prank calls were made from the church phones, and it became increasingly evident the program was perhaps more than the church had bargained for. But it was never more than we had. We worked harder, looked for inspiration and were never short on motivation.

We were definitely enjoying every moment of every day. We had time to concentrate on the eight children who were still at home. We decided that with everything we had been through, now was the perfect time for a family vacation. We ended up taking all ten of us on a cruise to Mexico. We had such an incredible time together. I do not think any of us had ever laughed that much in our lives. The kids did not even mind getting all dressed up each night for dinner, and they loved going to the shows. I think they had the most fun shopping in Mexico, though; they liked the whole concept of bargaining. We all were drawn to the ocean, snorkeling and boating. The mountains were beautiful, and all of us loved to ride horses. This was an incredibly healing trip for each of us.

We also loved going up to Avalanche Ranch; it was only about four hours west of us near Aspen in Red Feather. We would rent a huge ranch house and stay for four or five days. I loved to cook in the old wooden kitchen. We took many family hikes, we rode horses, and we even went for canoe rides in the dark of the night. We rode dirt bikes up and down the trails and spent quality time together. I felt that we were just beginning to get to know each other again. This was the first time we had no conflict; we were a family, and I loved who we had become.

The kids were involved in all kinds of sports. The boys played football during the fall with Joe as their coach and basketball in the winter, ran track and played baseball in the summer. The girls were cheerleaders and ran track. In between, they all became avid golfers. They also continued with swim and tennis lessons. I think I was most proud of the fact that no matter who had an event we all went. The kids supported one another; they were respectful of one another and genuinely wanted the best for each other. Many people commented on what an incredible family we were; they were not telling us anything we did not already know.

We had so much fun together. I loved practical jokes, always did and considered myself extremely good at them. I arranged many elaborate jokes for the kids, and they fell for them so many times. I did not wait for April Fool's Day. The kids never knew what to expect or when to expect it. Joe was also good at them. I remember one day he took the time to blow a dozen raw eggs out of their shells then put them back in their carton in the refrigerator. In the morning, as I began to make breakfast, I cracked one empty egg after another. I was confused. All I could think of was, I would need to take the eggs back to the store because they were empty. They all had a good laugh.

As the children grew older we paid the price, though, because they too became good at it. Once, when I was sitting in the orthodontist's office waiting for one of the children, Joey walked by me, my legs crossed, and quickly took my shoe. He then walked briskly to the hallway, put it on the elevator and sent it to who knew where. He sure had a good laugh at me hobbling out of the office. In the end each of them developed a great sense of humor. We laughed, we made each other laugh, and we shared that laughter with everyone.

For Christmas, Joe and I were torn about what to get them. Like most children they wanted for nothing. They had everything they needed and even more they did not. Finally we came up with the perfect idea. We placed one box for each of them under the Christmas tree. Then Joe would sneak in at night and change what was in the boxes to confuse them. One night he would fill them with nails, and the next maybe tissue; the boxes constantly changed. The kids were never so confused. Each of their boxes was exactly the same size, but each weighed a different amount and sounded different depending on the day. I loved watching their anticipation and excitement over the next couple of weeks.

On Christmas morning, as usual, they woke us early. We all gathered in front of the Christmas tree to open these mysterious boxes. Inside each was a letter. It read, "You have two hours; pack your things and be by the front door with your suitcase." The letter went on to give them a list of what they needed to bring but gave no indication of what was going to happen next.

Two hours later a huge twenty-passenger Hummer limousine pulled up in front of the house.

"Well, are you ready?" Joe asked.

They had question after question, all of which were wrapped with enthusiasm and excitement. Joe and I did not give away a thing; we just laughingly watched their exuberance. Soon we were all loaded in the limo and off to our Christmas adventure. About an hour out of town the limo pulled into an empty parking lot and came to a stop. The children were even more confused—until they saw their aunt and uncle's car pull up and their cousins jump out. They of course were equally confused as we told them to tell their parents good-bye and load their stuff in the limo.

We drove up the mountains about another hour until we finally reached Peaceful Valley Ranch, the destination for this mysterious journey. Joe and I planned a week of horse-drawn sleigh rides in the snow, swimming in the pools, ice-skating and snowmobiles. The boys had their own cabin, the girls had theirs, and Joe and I had our own; each had a huge hot tub in the front room. The kids had a great time sneaking up on each other's cabins and scaring one another. We played a giant game of "Survivor" that lasted the whole week, and Joe and I had so much fun coming up with immunity and reward challenges. It was great because hardly anyone else was up there; we had the place to ourselves.

The owners of the ranch made all the meals for us, so we really had no chores. The staff showed us how to play "ultimate ping-pong." We had never played before, but we loved it. We played game after game of ping-pong on the two tables that sat inside the large wooden gathering area. It was so beautiful and truly peaceful.

We had many adventures. We even went on another cruise. This one, although twice as long, ended far too soon. Each trip, each adventure, brought us closer together. We were beginning to experience the things I had always envisioned for us. It was not just the vacations that brought us happiness; it was the everyday life we had created. We were joyful, and our joy was evident to everyone who knew us.

Chapter Nine

To Teach and to Learn

Psalm 119:66
"Teach me knowledge and good judgment,
for I believe in your commands."

Those were great memories. I cherished them. Well, I did this day. I could not help but remember the joyful noise. With eight children, now becoming teenagers, along with all their friends, the house was never quiet. I missed that noise as I continued my work on the front porch. I looked over at the stereo, dusty and covered with leaves. I made it my next task to wash it as if it were brand new; I then turned it on. I have always loved music. Joe plays the guitar and banjo and has taught Joey and Paul to play as well. Mandy even took lessons. Our house was always filled with song, and I had no idea how much I missed it until I heard it again. Of all the changes I made to the porch this day, this may very well have been the grandest.

The kids were all doing fairly well in school. Their grades were good, they were popular, and we had no real behavior problems. But one day I received a phone call from Marissa's science teacher. She asked me when I was going to bring in Marissa's science project. I had no idea what she was talking about since I was not even aware Marissa had a project due. She said Marissa had informed her she had finished the project but could not take it on the bus, so I was going to bring it in and had not done that. She also mentioned that Marissa had lied to her on several other occasions. This was the first time I realized how good Marissa was at lying. A few other incidents happened, minor in nature but all pointing to the same thing: Marissa had secrets.

Joe and I were fully aware that everyone has secrets, and we have always been the type of parents who do not believe in invading the privacy of our children—unless they give us cause, and this was cause. I went up to Marissa's room and started to look through her things. In the top drawer of her desk she had a pile of notes. Some were from girlfriends, but the majority of them were from a boy named Malachi. I had never heard of Malachi before and had no idea who he was, but reading these letters assured me Marissa did know him and knew him well.

I do not know if I was relieved or more concerned when I came across a letter in which he informed her that either she would have sex with him or he was going to dump her for someone else. I was relieved she had not yet made that decision, but I was terribly concerned that the relationship had reached this point and we knew nothing of it. Our policy was no dating until they were sixteen unless it was in groups. Marissa had just turned sixteen and had not even asked to go on a date yet. The funny thing was, assuming all things were appropriate, we would have probably approved. We were not given that opportunity. She was spending time with him on her off-hour at school and when she was supposed to be at other places.

Joe and I decided to go down to her school. We asked the principal to open her locker for us, but we were in no way prepared for what we would find. We came across many papers on which she had forged my name. She was failing several classes and had signed our names to the Informed Parents' sheets. There was also evidence she had been skipping classes and having a friend "fix" the attendance slips at the office. Then Joe came across a cassette tape; he put it in the tape player that was also in her locker and listened. It was from Malachi, and he was asking Marissa to run away from home with him.

Joe and I knew that whatever we did we needed to do it quickly because she was about to make a decision that would affect the rest of her life. With little conversation, we both agreed. We needed to take her out of school, and I needed to home school her to get her back to where she needed to be and keep her from making some terribly wrong choices. We went to the office and withdrew her from school, and then we went to her classroom. I do not know what she was thinking when we got there. We had taken the children out of school for surprise jaunts before, but I think she knew this was more serious. It was only when she asked if she could go to her locker that we told her the truth.

The next few days were filled with our trying to get information on how to home school a high school student. We went to District Admissions and filed the paperwork as to the expectations and requirements. We developed a curriculum and went to the bookstore to purchase the syllabus, the texts and even the tests and answers. Joe and I were inquisitive and tried to learn all we could. Marissa never spoke a word; she was not rude or disrespectful to us, but she was angry, and she was sad.

We called Malachi, spoke with him and his mother, and informed them that Marissa and he were to have no contact until she got back on track with her schoolwork. Then altogether we would sit down and figure out where to go from there. I am sure she missed him. I am sure she missed her freedom, and I am equally sure she was apprehensive about how this could work.

Weeks passed, and slowly so did her anger. At first she was certain she would not engage with me and she would make sure this did not work. In time she conceded, and before long we were both enjoying each other's company. We had so much time together. We completed the school-work, and then we took walks, we talked, and we spent a lot of time really getting to know each other. We talked about Malachi and about boys in general. We talked about secrets and even about running away. I felt that she had been drawn into something that was way over her head, and the more she considered it, the more she understood what a mistake it all was.

I missed the time I had to myself, but it did not take long for me to realize this was one of our best decisions. I had so looked forward to the time when Johnny would start first grade because I could not imagine what it would feel like to have them all in school. Ironically he was now in school, but she was not. I laughed sometimes, and sometimes I cried, but in the end it was the right thing to do.

A couple of months later Amy left a note for me when she went to school; this was not unusual for the kids to do. Sometimes they would leave a sweet little note saying they loved us, and sometimes they would leave something more serious. I guess they thought writing a note was less scary than having to tell us something difficult, and for Amy this was difficult.

She wrote of how unhappy she was at school and how she did not feel as if she fit in. She begged me to withdraw her and allow her to be home schooled. She assured me she could learn much more from me than she could from the school. She asked me to pray about it and decide quickly, she wrote, because she was so sad.

I did pray about it, and so did Joe. In the end we allowed her to leave public school and join Marissa in the home school. This was a defining point in Amy's and my relationship. I had always said I did not feel as if I really knew who she was; it was difficult to get through to her. She had built her own walls, and I was sure the reason we could not figure out who she was, was that she had no idea herself. That was where we would need to begin.

I wanted to get to know her. I made time for us to be alone and talk about everything from silly to serious to tragic. I wanted to know her opinion on friendship, on family, on politics, on religion, on life. I wanted her to develop her own opinions separate from Marissa and the other children. I wanted her to get to know herself and in turn share that with me; to my absolute joy, she did.

We look back on our parenting, and we see the things we have done right as well as our mistakes. In the end I guess the best we can hope for is that what we do well outweighs what we do not. I made many mistakes with Amy, but this was not one of them. I consider this time with her a gift, one I was not even worthy of. I had no idea what an incredible woman she was becoming. The truth was, she did have opinions; she just did not have the self-esteem to share them. As she felt better about herself and opened up to me, I was daily amazed at the depth of her assessments of life.

She was passionate about political issues, as was I, so we loved to debate. We watched CNN for fun and had philosophical discussions on everything. She was passionate about her faith and, through her questioning, caused me to become more introspective and insightful. We brought out the best in each other.

We started with walks every day. The walks became longer, and then one was not enough; we were always together. Mandy and Joe had gone on long walks each night; they had so much to discuss. Mandy, in most ways, is so much like her father. I always envied their time together, but they saw the world through the same eyes. Now it was Amy's and my time. The walks were filled with constant conversation. I fell in love with her on the walking path, and I believe she did with me as well. I could not believe we had wasted all these years, without really knowing who each was. Now that we knew, we were inseparable. As a bonus she lost a few pounds, and so her self-esteem increased—well, that and the fact that she got her braces off, began wearing contacts instead of glasses and her hair grew long. She became absolutely beautiful. Amanda always had been, and Amy grew into it. She was gorgeous, and she finally believed it herself. This newfound outward beauty gave her the chance to be more vocal with others about what she believed on the inside. What at first she would only share with me, she was now ready for the whole world to hear. She never stopped talking after that.

I look back on those days, and I cannot help but thank God. Marissa and I enjoyed home schooling, but Amy and I needed it. Soon Paul too decided he wanted to be home schooled; this only lasted one semester. He missed sports and hanging out with the other guys at lunchtime; I sensed he missed the girls as well. All three of the children attended a Friday school designed for home-school students to have the opportunity to interact with other home-school students. Great in concept and maybe in theory, this particular one was not so good in practical application or possibly, it was just a difficult transition for the children to make. Paul returned to public school, and Amy and Marissa continued with home school; but they all quit Friday school.

Life was happy. Amanda was attending a private Christian high school for girls, and she was preparing to graduate. It was difficult for both Joe and me to comprehend that our oldest child was now preparing for college. She was an awesome student, was on the golf team, and played basketball for her high school. At this time she decided to become a doctor, although Joe and I had always known she would. As a child she had not been fascinated by the outward beauty of anything, not even a bird; she was always intrigued with the inner—what made it live.

She was sure of herself and her life—at least that was what she portrayed. I am certain that like all teenagers she had mixed feelings; she just was not going to let anyone know about them. I thought it would be so difficult for her to leave and move out on her own, but not so. She was strong, independent, and ready to go; that made it easier for us to let her go.

Joey was also at a private Christian high school—his, of course, for boys. He played football and basketball and ran track for the school. He had always been a great athlete, and now was his chance to shine; he took it. This was about more than sports though, for he was developing into a young man of character with a deep and compassionate faith. He had won the character award at his school; they too saw what we did. He was also preparing for college and decided he wanted to go into business with his father. This made sense because he was becoming just like his father, not just handsome, but a good and kind man of faith, who also had a love for business.

Colton struggled academically; there was no denying that. He was lucky because his good looks, charm and charisma often got him out of sticky situations at school. He too was an incredible athlete, not so much because he wanted to be but more because of his competitiveness with Joey. Colton never had any behavior problems at school, which contributed to his acceptance at the private high school Joey attended. Joe and I were never quite sure if he truly wanted to go there or if he wanted to because Joey did. In the end it did not matter; we were all so excited when he was tentatively accepted. He had to attend summer school, but he was in. He did fine that first year. He lettered in wrestling and was a star on the football team; he also ran track. His grades were not great, but they kept him eligible. Most of all he was well liked by the teachers, the staff and his peers.

Willy also struggled; his problem was not inability. Willy had spent those early years not getting to be a kid. Now that he had the opportunity, he was going to take it. He was silly and immature and liked to be the center of attention. He had a good sense of humor and made everyone around him laugh. Unfortunately he did the same in school. It seemed both Joe and I were constantly at his school; his poor teachers were at their wits' end. Will knew what was expected of him; he just loved life and was going to let everyone know that.

We had a similar experience with Marissa. She had not been allowed to fully enjoy her childhood and was now taking advantage of it. When she was twelve and thirteen she still loved playing with Barbie and Barbie's friends; she would play with them for hours. She also loved playing with baby dolls. She would ask me sometimes if I thought she was too old to play with her toys. I always told her there was no such thing; often I played with her. She needed to be a child; no one had ever let her do that; now was her time. Willy understood that because it was also his time.

The main word that comes to mind when thinking of Johnny during this time is inconsistent. After he had attended the therapeutic preschool, he seemed to make some real progress. He had begun to trust me and was making a real effort to abide by our expectations. But when he went to public school for kindergarten that all changed. He became secretive, distrustful, manipulative and solitary. At times, of course, he was happy and engaged, but over the next years we would see those times become more and more overshadowed by the darker side of his personality. I wonder if we had known his secret then, could all that happened later have been avoided?

Chapter Ten

The Kiss of Betrayal

As I reminisced, I picked up the rose clippers and began the tedious job of pruning back each individual branch that had not been able to withstand the harshness it had encountered. I stopped at the vines that had the will to survive and wondered why it was that under the exact same conditions some lived and some died. What made the difference?

This made me wonder further if our survival, and ultimately our new growth, is merely a choice or if we are somehow destined in our response. I do not know why the answer was so important to me now, but as I laid each stem down that had not survived, I could not help but question if anything could have made a difference, and so the memories continued.

Tuesday, August 26, 2003, became the day that would change our lives forever. A frantic knock on our bedroom door awoke us. It was Amy calling out in a panicky voice, "Marissa is gone!"

"What?" Joe replied.

"Marissa is gone. She is not in her bed, and I've looked all over the house. She is gone."

I jumped from the bed and grabbed my robe. I followed Amy back into Marissa's room, and she was not there. I looked around for a moment trying to make some sense out of this. I thought to myself, are her clothes here? What about her books—are they still here? Did she leave on her own free will? Where could she be?

Just then William ran through the doorway and said, "Colton is not in his room either."

I had to sit down—rather I collapsed onto the edge of the bed. This had to be a dream, no, more likely a nightmare. I kept questioning, I thought to myself, but maybe I was asking out loud: Where could they be, and why would they leave? By now, all the children had gathered in Marissa's room, and Joe was there too. I had to find the strength to stand back up. I needed to comfort the other children, and I needed to find Colton and Marissa. I was sure they needed me.

We all hurried down the stairs to Colton's room to see if his things were missing. To our dismay they were. His large red athletic bag was gone as were many of his clothes, his jeans, shirts and his jacket. I checked for his cell phone and his bankcard; they too were gone. By then I was fighting back the tears. I had to face the unbearable realization that they had left on their own. No one had broken into our home; no one had stolen our children. They had left me, us, our family, and there was no apparent reason why.

The next thing I knew we were all in the kitchen, looking at each other in shock, each of us enduring our own confusion. Amy blurted out, "Let's call Colton's cell phone."

"Yes!" we all agreed in unison.

I grabbed the phone and anxiously dialed his number. It went straight to voice mail.

"Colton, where are you, baby? I am so worried about you. What happened? Please call me. Whatever it is, we can work it out. I need you to call, please, please. . . ."

We called maybe ten times, each of us taking our turn beseeching him to call us. Then someone had the idea to call the bank and see if he had taken out money. I picked up the phone to make the first of what would be endless embarrassing phone calls.

I began, "Hello, my son has an account there, and I cannot find him, and I need to know if he took any money out." The woman on the other end was kind, she sensed my distress, and I felt her compassion.

"Yes, Mrs. Hannah, he was here at 6:00 a.m. to withdraw money from the ATM."

Quickly I looked at the clock; it was 6:40. If they were walking, they could not have gotten far.

I ran to the car. I felt someone behind me. I could not take the time to turn and look. When I got in, Joey opened the passenger door and jumped in. "I'm going along," he said. I did not protest; I was happy he was with me but sad because I wanted to break down and knew I could not do that in front of him. Instead we needed to find them. We drove aimlessly until eventually we both faced the fact that they must have had some kind of vehicle. We were not going to find them; we needed to go home.

When we opened the garage door, all the kids ran out. "Did you find them? Where are they?" they cried. I felt that I had failed them; it was my job as mom to know where my children were. Where were they?

"No, we couldn't find them," I said softly. Their faces dropped, and we stood in a silence that was deafening.

We went into the kitchen where we held hands and prayed, each of us taking our turn. By now it was almost 7:30; the kids needed to go to school. Joe assured them we would find Colton and Marissa. They should go on to school, and we would take care of it. He even told them to call home from school if they wanted to and we would give them an update; all would be fine. I looked at Joe and could not help but wonder if he truly believed that or if he was saying it only for their benefit. Either way it worked and the children headed off to school.

"We have to get a shower and go find them," I whispered. Joe agreed. We showered and prepared for the day without another word. When we were ready we sat down in the kitchen and tried to analyze the situation; we tried to figure out what had happened.

"Well, Colton obviously packed a bag. It must have been planned," I said.

"I found a bag in Marissa's room packed with several outfits of clothes," Joe said, "actually an odd choice in clothes. She had a couple of dresses and some nice outfits, no jeans or T-shirts. The bag also contained all her makeup and curling iron. She obviously had thought this through. The only thing I don't understand is why she did not take the bag."

"Maybe she heard someone coming or for some reason had to leave quickly and forgot it," I answered.

"Maybe, but she did not take her car, her car keys, her bank card, anything. It looks as if Marissa just walked out the door."

"The door—how did they get out?" I asked.

We jumped up and went back down the basement stairs to Colton's room. We checked the window. The screen was standing against the wall, behind the bed, and the security chains on the window were unlocked. It was obvious from the leaves that had been disturbed that they had left through this window.

I sat down again on the bed, put my face in my hands and finally wept, not knowing if I would ever be able to stop. But something happened that made me stop; it was the sudden realization that I was sitting on Willy's bed. I was startled to think that Colton and Marissa could have crawled over his sleeping body and out the window without saying so much as "good-bye." He was their brother. Willy had lost his mother and his father; they had to know he could not survive his only biological brother and sister abandoning him as well, especially in his sleep. They could not be that cruel—no one could—or at least I thought. At that point we knew we needed to find them. Obviously we would search because of our love and concern for them, but we also had to do this for Willy.

I remember thinking we should call someone, but not knowing whom we should call. I did not want to call the school and report Colton absent. I was sure he would be back this morning, and I did not want to get him in trouble at school. I was convinced this was just a mistake, one we could handle here. I eventually decided there was no need to get the school involved. So instead we headed for the car; we would find them on our own.

We drove for hours. We had no idea where to go; we just drove. We prayed, we questioned everything that could have happened to them, and we drove. Before we knew it, it was late afternoon. The kids would be home from school soon, and we needed to get back. When we arrived home, we decided it was time to call the sheriff's department. We did, and when we told them our sixteen- and seventeen-year-old children had run away they transferred us to voice mail. We left a message; it was all we could do.

The other children returned from school, and we had the painful task of telling them we had not found their brother and sister. That night we worked through different scenarios in our mind of what could have happened; none of them made any sense. It was only the fourth day of school for Colton; he had been so excited to go back. Football season had begun, and even Colton was aware of what an awesome player he was. We had not fought, not had even a minor disagreement. In fact the night before, Colton had come into my room to kiss me good night and said, "Mom, on Saturday can we go out on a date day, just you and me?"

"Sure," I replied, "just you and me."

With that, he hugged me and gave me a kiss. Could that have been the kiss of betrayal? I was not yet ready to believe that.

What about Marissa? Why would she run away? We had argued the day before. I had taken her cell phone away because she was not being honest about it, but that surely would not be enough reason to run away. She was excited to start her community college courses, which we had registered for only the week prior, and she enjoyed her job. She was looking forward to turning eighteen in only a few months. She seemed excited about her future. Even though she was angry, this did not make sense. She had come to my room the night before to say good night, and she too told me she loved me.

None of our scenarios made sense. In the end we were probably more confused than we were when the conversation began. We knelt down around the table, held hands and prayed again. This time our prayers were less shock and more confusion. We asked God for answers, but we felt none. Sadly we hugged and kissed good night, and we each headed off to our own rooms to endure a sleepless night.

The next day was the same as the day before. We awoke, we prayed, and we searched for them and for answers. Each time we returned home, I was sure I would see them sitting on the front porch, in the rocking chairs, waiting for us. They would then tell us they were sorry and had made a terrible mistake. We would just forgive them and go back to our lives. They would not explain; there could be no reasonable explanation. They would embrace us, and our children would be home. That never happened, and the incredible sorrow became overwhelming.

The sheriff finally returned our call. He took the report over the phone. He was not overly concerned.

"It happens all the time," he said. "They will show up; just give it some time."

It may happen all the time, but it had never happened to us. We felt devastated by the lack of support. We did not know what to do. It was as if we were in a dream and did not know how to wake up, even though we were desperate to do so. We were wearing down, engulfed in sadness and uncertainty. "God, what should we do?" That was our last prayer before bed.

When we awoke on Thursday morning, I felt God had answered our prayer. The answer was that Marissa and Colton were gone, and there were things Joe and I needed to do. We needed to take control of the situation; we had to be strong for the whole family. In some ways we were thankful we could at least keep busy this day, even though we were sure the tasks at hand would be both humiliating and embarrassing. The first stop was the bank. We closed both the checking accounts and savings accounts of each of them. I was grateful that when we opened them we had our names put on the accounts along with theirs; now there would be no more money.

Next stop, school—Colton had to be withdrawn. This was a private Christian school, and even if he returned there was no doubt he would be expelled. We knew we had to do it, but it still turned out to be more difficult than we had anticipated. We went to the office and explained; I could not hold back the tears. The woman in the office looked at me as if she felt my pain but had no idea what to say. There were no words of comfort—only papers to fill out, a locker to clean out and his teachers to speak with about what had happened. Finally they directed us to the athletic department to have

Colton's football locker emptied. I cried again, or maybe I was still crying; I do not remember if I ever stopped.

The boys in the hall saw us. One boy said, "Hey, Mr. and Mrs. Hannah, how's it going?"

It was impossible for us to answer. It was almost a blessing when the other boys looked away. As we walked out the door, I felt my legs give way, and I wondered if I could make it to the car. When Joe opened the door, the emotion I had been controlling overcame me. I grieved for Colton, but I grieved for my dreams for him as well. I had worked so hard to help him get into this school. I wanted this for him; I had always wanted every opportunity for him. He needed this; he could succeed here. But now that dream was gone. Four days ago he was a sophomore at the top high school in Colorado, an exceptional athlete and an incredible son. Now he was a sixteen-year-old runaway and high school dropout. The pain was incredible.

Fortunately we had more work to do. We had to go to Marissa's job and talk with her boss. We had to cancel both of their cell phones. We had to revoke Marissa's driver's license and cancel her car insurance. If we could limit their capabilities, maybe they would come home. This was the hope we clung to through yet another sleepless night.

Friday morning we received a phone call from Colton's football coach. He was the first one to call and offer his concern and his support. I did my best not to cry through the entire conversation. He told me he would do everything he could to help. He went on to say he would keep the players in after practice and talk with them. He assured me that if they knew anything he would find out. We did not hold out much hope, and this turned out to be a very dreary and bleak day.

Paul and Willy had football practice that afternoon, and since Joe was one of the coaches, we knew we had to get it together enough to go. It turned out to be a good idea; attending a regular activity seemed to offer some semblance of normality. Colton's coach called during practice; he had some information. The week prior to Colton's running away, several players had seen him after practice in the parking lot. He was at a white pick-up truck with a tall thin blonde girl, and they seemed intimately involved. They had seen her around practice for a few days, and one player knew who she was. Her name was Desiree Connor, and she attended the local public high school. The coach went on to say that he felt she must know something.

We hurried home and called the Connor residence. We had the number from our church directory. I had met Desiree only once when Joe and I hosted the church youth party prior to their leaving for the mission trip. I had met her mother briefly. I knew nothing really of the family but was thankful it was someone from our church.

Joe called the Connor house. Desiree's mother answered the phone, and Joe told her about our situation. He informed her that Desiree had been seen with Colton and that she must know something; he then asked to speak with her. Desiree's mother assured Joe she had no information but would keep us in her prayers, and then she gave the phone to Desiree. Joe told her in a humble and shaken voice that any information she could give us could help bring Colton home. Desiree seemed extremely willing to help, even cried and told Joe she had no idea where either Marissa or Colton were, and certainly she would tell us if she did. Joe hung up with no more information or answers than he had prior to the call.

We felt the lead was dead; Amy did not. She could not let it go; she felt Desiree knew something. Unbeknownst to us she went upstairs and called Desiree back. I am not sure what she said, but about an hour later Desiree called back and told Amy that she did, in fact, have information. She went on to say, "I saw Colton and Marissa today after school. They were with a big black man, and they seemed to be with him against their will. They are staying in an apartment in a dangerous area; they snuck out of the apartment tonight to call me." Desiree began to cry and then said, "I am just as worried about them as you are. I will call you as soon as they call me tomorrow, which they promised they would."

Now we had gone from no information to some that was very disturbing. We wondered who this man was and how Colton and Marissa could not escape from him when they could make it out of the apartment to phone Desiree. None of this made any sense.

Needless to say, this was our worst night. We were confused and saddened prior to this, but we had not felt that either of them was in any real danger. Now we did. I do not ever remember sleeping that night. By sunrise Joe and I just lay in bed, not wanting to let each other go. Every minute seemed like hours, and there seemed to be no end to our pain. We were startled by the sound of the phone ringing. Joe answered, and it was Desiree's mom. She said, "I have some news, but I need to talk with you alone. I will meet you at Village Inn in half an hour and I will tell you what I know. One more thing—do not bring your wife."

Joe hung up with a stunned look on his face. He told me what she had said. I was confused; I could not understand why I was not allowed to go. Nevertheless, I accepted it. We needed any information she had for us; no matter who she decided was worthy to receive it. Joe showered, dressed and left hurriedly. He was gone about an hour, but it seemed more like days. The phone finally rang; I knew it was him.

"What—what did she know?" I asked.

"Deb, you are not going to believe this. Colton and Marissa have been staying at her house the entire time. She has been hiding them out."

"No, no," I said. "We called her last night. She said she didn't know."

"It gets worse, Deb," he interrupted. "She is not the only one who knew where they were. Pastor Thomas knew. She had spoken with him on Thursday and told him of the entire situation, and he did nothing."

I heard the words, but I could not process them. "What?" I kept asking. "What are you saying?"

"I am saying that Pastor Thomas knew where the kids were, but he was leaving on a camping trip for the Labor Day Holiday. So he talked it over with his assistant, Julie, and they decided not to act on it."

"Julie," I said. "I had lunch with her only last week. There is no way that as a mother she could have kept this from me. She would not have done that."

"Deb, she did. They both did," he replied.

Nothing seemed real. All I knew to be true was dissipating in front of me. What was happening?

"Deb, are you there?"

Through my tears I answered, "Yes."

"There's more. The reason I was asked to come alone is that both Colton and Marissa are claiming they were physically abused by you and ran away from home for their own safety. Desiree's mom said she kept the kids to keep them safe from you."

I fell to the bed. "Does she believe that? She knows me. How could she believe that? How could any of them believe that?"

"I'll be home in a minute," Joe said, "and we will work this out." I just paced until he arrived.

When he came in he embraced me. "Deb, we know where they are. They're safe. Let's just keep our focus on that."

"I want my kids back. I want them home," I interrupted. "She can't keep them. It's against the law. There is a law about contributing to the delinquency of a minor or something, isn't there? We need to call the sheriff."

Joe agreed and made the call. The sheriff said we should try to talk with the kids and get them home. If it did not work, he would go over there and pick them up.

We called Desiree's house, and Colton and Marissa both spoke with us reluctantly. All I asked was that they meet us, if only for a few minutes, and let us talk with them. We told them we would not force them to come home if they would just meet us. Halfheartedly they agreed. They wanted to meet at the church. I found this surprising. I did not think anyone would be at the church to let us in at that time, so Joe suggested Dairy Queen. They covered the phone, obviously to talk it over, and then said they would be there in a few minutes.

I hung up the phone, and Joe and I headed for the door. The phone rang again. This time it was Desiree's stepfather. "Why are you making such a big deal out of this?" he said. "Kids run away all the time. Desiree has run away a lot; sometimes kids just need a place they can crash until they get over it. I did you a favor by keeping them."

I was shocked. "Do you know what we have been through these last five days?" I asked. "We had no idea where our children were. How can you act so cavalier?"

He laughed; he actually laughed. Our pain and our sorrow were nothing more than a joke to him. I hung up because this was not about him; I had to go see my children.

Joe and I raced to the car and headed toward Dairy Queen. When we pulled into the parking lot we saw our pastor, Thomas, pull up in the church van and head in to talk with Colton and Marissa. By this time I had no idea what was real anymore. As I walked in the door I snapped at him, "What are you doing here?"

As I brushed by him he said something to the effect of "Can we just talk about this?"

"No, just leave us alone. I want to see my children." My voice was loud and stern. Only yesterday I had considered this man my friend; now I did not know who he was. My heart was broken.

He looked at Joe and asked if he could speak to him outside. Joe agreed and followed. I sat down with Colton and Marissa. I held their hands and asked them why they had left. Marissa did not answer.

Colton finally said, "We're grown up. We always knew we would leave; now is the time. I want to be with Desiree. We want to be together, and her parents don't mind. Marissa likes hanging out over there too."

"What about school?" I asked. They both put their heads down and did not answer. I asked, "Colton, did you get the phone messages?"

"Yea," he said.

"You knew the pain we were in, and you left us there."

"Yea."

"What about Willy?" I asked. Again there was no answer.

Joe returned about then and sat down. He was visibly shaken. He looked at Colton and Marissa and said, "What happened?" Again there was no reply. Joe then asked, "Do you want to come home?" This time there was an answer.

"No, we want to be on our own," Marissa said, and Colton agreed. At this point I began to beg and plead with them to come home. They looked at each other, and Marissa said, "We made a decision before we came here today that we were not going to come home, and we don't want to go back on that decision now."

"I don't understand," I said. "Why did you leave?"

"We are grown up," Colton replied again, "and we knew you would still make us stay in school and you wouldn't let us live with Desiree."

I asked one more time. "Come home for just a few days, and let's try to work this through." Once again there was no answer. It was becoming increasingly clear these were not the children we had known only days before. They were distant, detached and not willing to pretend they were anything different. We talked a few more minutes, and then they said they needed to go. Joe asked one more time if they would come home. They looked down and did not answer. I could not bear the pain any longer, and I could not bear to see the deep pain on Joe's face either. We stood up and walked out the door. I glanced back once; they were still looking down.

Joey, Amy, Paul and William were waiting by the door when we returned. We told them what had happened. Oddly they did not seem overly upset. We told them Colton and Marissa were not coming home, and there were no tears. I think they were trying to be strong for Joe and me. We discussed the situation and decided Colton and Marissa could choose not to come home, but we were not letting them stay there with a woman who would lie to their parents to protect them. We called the sheriff again and gave him an update.

I then emailed the pastor. I would be lying if I said Joe and I were not completely surprised by the lack of support. We considered this church our home. We did all the things you do for the people you consider your extended family. When Pastor Thomas's dad moved out to Colorado, Joe arranged for his subcontractors as well as for himself to work on the home. On their own time they converted part of the garage into an additional bedroom. Even though it was an extensive remodel, Joe never considered not volunteering his time; it was simply what you do.

Sadly, after Pastor Thomas's dad moved out here his situation deteriorated rapidly, resulting in a stroke that totally debilitated him. I was visiting with him when I could, taking him out in his wheelchair for walks or just spending time with him. After the stroke, the girls and I continued to visit with him at the hospital and then nursing home. All the while we made meals regularly and took them to the family. We never considered not helping; it is what you hope anyone would do when your family is in a time of crisis. Little did we know our time of crisis was so close at hand.

In the email I was now writing I expressed my bewilderment that as a friend of this family he could have allowed us to endure this kind of pain. He knew us; he knew me. I had run the after-school program for two years; he knew how I was with children. He knew my heart and would certainly know I was not capable of abusing these children. He knew our family and how much we loved and adored each of our children and how each of them was flourishing.

I then wrote that barring all that, if by some chance, he still believed it possible, he should have reported it to Social Services so we would have at least known where our children were; the law stated he must. I asked why he did nothing when he should have at least contacted us and told us they were safe or even referred it to the youth pastor whom all the children had learned to trust, and then he could have intervened. I am sure I wrote much more. I was typing so fast and so full of anger.

I then sent an email to Julie; it was pretty much the same. I was not as personally familiar with her, but I knew she had always taken a very legalistic approach to the church. So my note to her centered on the legal responsibilities of the church in reporting the delinquency of a minor and the suspected child abuse. Our state requires mandatory reporting. I went on to write that Joe and I held her and the church liable for this failure to report.

Betrayal of trust creates a dichotomy of anger and overwhelming emotional pain. We were now experiencing both. I suppose the only people who can really hurt us are the ones we allow ourselves to care for deeply. Pastor Thomas really hurt us.

Joe was sure there must be some kind of mistake. Surely a man he considered a friend could not have known where our children were the last few days and have decided to do nothing. He called Pastor Thomas to seek answers. I heard him say, "Father to father, friend to friend, how could you have allowed this to happen? If you had told us when you first knew, you could have prevented so much of our grief—and we could have prevented Colton's expulsion from school and much of the nightmare that followed."

I did not hear Pastor Thomas's response, but Joe told me later he had simply said, "They were claiming abuse. I felt it was a family matter and decided it best not to get involved. At this time I don't think I owe you an apology." With that all the years of friendship dissolved. We had been there for him and his family in their time of need. This in no way obligated him to us, but we thought the years of friendship had.

We never heard another word from Pastor Thomas, Julie, the youth pastor or any of the people with whom we had shared the last few years. It is true that I chose to stop communicating with them by email, it seemed so pointless, but I always expected the phone to ring or the doorbell to chime and it would be one of them. It never was. It is difficult to say why, maybe there was some concern we would seek legal action, maybe they really believed Marissa and Colton, or maybe they just did not want to be involved. The reason does not really matter, because all things are justifiable; but not all things are right.

The rest of the night felt similar to a wake. It was as if we had lost two children—only they were not dead; they were just lost to us. I lay in bed and prayed; I begged God to take this from us. I drifted off to sleep for a few minutes and dreamt I was speaking with God. He too was saddened and assured me He never wanted this for our family. He assured me it was His pain as well, and I felt His comfort when I awoke in remembering the words of Agathon, "This only is denied to God: the power to undo the past."

It was Sunday. Oddly, we did not speak of Colton and Marissa. We were so drained from the previous week, and each of us needed a moment away from it; but inwardly our hearts were broken. About 4:00 p.m. Joe was in the back cleaning out the hot tub when the phone rang; he answered it outside. It was Desiree. She said Colton and Marissa wanted to come home, and they wanted us to come and pick them up at a homeless shelter in downtown Denver. Joe told her that if Colton and Marissa wanted to come home they would have to call us themselves; he hung up. The phone rang again in a few minutes, and it was Colton. He simply said, "We are ready to come home. We are at a mission in downtown Denver. Can we come home?"

"We will be right there. We'll talk about it then," Joe quickly answered.

I was so caught up in the moment I do not even remember looking around the room to see how the other children were responding to the news. In retrospect, I should have. Instead we raced out the door to save Colton and Marissa.

It took us about forty-five minutes to drive to the shelter. I wondered how Colton and Marissa had made their way that far. If the sheriff had made them leave Desiree's house last night, where had they been? I was full of questions, but my main concern was having my children home.

As we pulled up to the building, I was surprised. Not only did it look abandoned, but it also looked as if it had been so for a long time. Colton and Marissa were sitting out front. They could not have looked more out of place. There they were, these two blond, well-dressed, well-spoken kids sitting on the curb, with of all things Colton's Barney sleeping bag. It was an odd sight.

They jumped in the car and told us how scared they were that we would not come. They said repeatedly how sorry they were. We told them we would stop and get something to eat and then try to figure out where to go from here. We stopped at a nearby restaurant. I was surprised when they did not order; they said they were not hungry. I knew they should be but dismissed it as emotion.

After we ordered we began to ask them some questions. They said Desiree's family had put them out after the sheriff came because they did not want to be involved. They went on to say they had spent the last night in the park, and it was raining so hard that they had not slept at all. Finally at sunrise they were so cold that they just started walking and walked all day until they got to the shelter downtown. They said that when they got to the shelter they talked about it and decided they really wanted to come home. They said they had heard gunshots and were afraid of the people playing basketball there because they were sure they were gang members. Together and separately they told us what a terrible mistake they had made and how much they wanted to come home. Colton said he had been so taken in by Desiree and wanted to be with her all the time, but now he and Desiree were through. He said he had found out about the real Desiree while he was gone, and he was finished with her. We believed him; we believed both of them. They were our children, and in some ways we needed to.

I remember stroking Marissa's hair, and as I lifted it, it was wet underneath. It was like when you wash your hair and put it up while it is still wet and it never dries underneath. I was almost sure I smelled shampoo. I asked her about it, but she said it was simply wet from the rain in the park. I remember Marissa accidentally saying they had lunch at Applebee's. This was odd because that was here on our end of town not on the way to the shelter. I asked them how they knew the directions to the shelter, and they said they had just asked people along the way. There were inconsistencies in what they said—many in fact. I just don't think we were ready yet to face the truth.

We brought Colton and Marissa home. Again something seemed strange. The other children did not run to greet either of them; instead they showed no happiness or even relief that their brother and sister were home. I could understand, I thought. Joey and Colton went to school together and played on the same football team. He was angry at the embarrassment and shame Colton had brought on him. Amy and Marissa were so close; she must have been devastated that Marissa could have hurt her that way. In addition Amy had begun attending the first multi-campus Jesuit high school in the nation. After being the first girl accepted, this was her time; now they had taken this from her as well. Then there was William. Of course William would be angry, but I was not yet sure why Paul was.

Marissa sat on the floor, held William in her lap and told him she would never ever leave him again. She told him it was her promise, and he could believe it. I am not sure if he did; he made no indication either way.

We contacted the sheriff's department to report that Colton and Marissa had returned home. He informed us it was protocol for him to come back out and interview Colton and Marissa about what had happened; that afternoon he did. He listened to their whole story, and I recall being slightly upset because he did not seem to believe them. I just wanted the past to be the past and to move on from here. He sternly told them that if it happened again he could have them declared beyond our reasonable control and have them placed outside the home. They seemed frightened, and I was sure they would never do something like that again.

They were home; they were safe. Unfortunately we were still their parents and of course needed to implement some consequence for what had happened. They each lost privileges for the next thirty days. They lost their cell phones, use of the car and even their rooms. They had to share the loft with much less privacy for the thirty days.

We also told them that since Monday was a holiday, Labor Day, we would enroll them in school on Tuesday. They would both be enrolled in public school. Colton said he was scared and asked if I would go in with him, talk to the counselor and help him get his books and settle in. Not only did I go, but Joe did as well. We even signed him up for football again. We wanted him to have his life back.

While we were at the school with Colton and Marissa, Joe received a call on his cell phone. It was from the Department of Social Services. The caseworker said that a complaint had come in Saturday afternoon claiming I had physically abused Colton and Marissa as well as Johnny and Willy. The anonymous caller had said I beat the children and they were in fear for their lives. He went on to say that, Social Services took this report very seriously and he would need to come to our house that afternoon. He further said we needed to have all the children home from school because each would need to be interviewed alone to find the underlying cause of these allegations.

He arrived at our home about 3:30. He interviewed each of the children separately in the other room. First to be interviewed was Joey who had to come home from football practice, then Amy, Paul, William, Johnny, Amanda, and Colton and Marissa. Finally he got to Joe and me. He decided also to interview us separately. He asked about all the forms of discipline we used, the rules of the house, and our feelings toward Colton and Marissa. He said the complaint made against us was vague and unclear but would be fully investigated. He looked through the entire house, made his notes and told us we would hear from them in a few days. Later we found out the allegations had been determined to be unfounded, and we were cleared.

At home things had settled down. We began to talk about what happened. Colton and I spent hours discussing where to go from here. We discussed his plans and his future. He seemed so cooperative. He listened, he acted respectful, and he seemed to want our advice. Finally I had to ask, "Colton, how could you have let people you love go through so much?"

"I just never thought about it," he said. "I was busy doing other things. We went out to dinner with Desiree's parents. Desiree, Marissa and I went to the movies together. We played with their dogs, and we had a lot of fun. We just never thought about you."

"Colton, were you there the night Dad and I called and Desiree's mom said she had not seen you?"

"Yes, that's what we decided to say." Colton shrugged.

"I don't understand. Why did you say you were abused?"

"We would not have been able to get them to let us stay there if we did not say that," Colton answered.

It was unfathomable that such a simple answer was all that was needed to explain such a heartbreaking betrayal. It was incomprehensible that anyone could hurt someone he or she claimed to love in such a way and yet feel no remorse. He, as well as Marissa, dismissed our pain. I remember this moment as the first time I realized there was something terribly wrong.

The kids went back to school. We knew Desiree was attending this same school, but we had Colton's assurance he did not even want to speak with her. In fact, he asked for my help in writing a letter to Desiree telling her it was over. Marissa told us she would be with Colton when he gave it to her, and she would make sure nothing ever happened between them again. When they returned from school they both said Desiree was crying in school all day because she was so upset that Colton had broken up with her.

The days went on, and things seemed to be healing. Colton and Marissa had accepted their consequences for their actions. They were accountable for each moment of their time and arrived home exactly when they were supposed to each day. Colton had football practice after school so he did not get home until about 6:00. Marissa would always come straight home from school.

It was now late September. Colton had a football game that Saturday. He had not been able to play in the previous games because he had to have a certain number of practices in before he was allowed to play. Colton said he did not want us to come because he was sure he would not get much playing time since he had been there only a few weeks. Joey, Paul and William had a football game that day as well, so we were not sure how we could make it to all of them.

Joey's game ended early so Joe and Amanda decided they would surprise Colton and go to his game. Even if he did not get to play much, the important thing was that they show their support. When they arrived they did not see Colton on the field. After a few minutes they approached the coach and asked him where Colton was.

The coach looked perplexed. "Colton, Colton who?"

"Colton Hannah. He just started here three weeks ago," Joe answered.

"Oh, that Colton. We haven't seen him. He has never showed up to practice, and he is not on the team. We knew he registered, and that is the last we heard of him."

Joe and Amanda walked away with the shame and embarrassment that had become part of who we were. They came home and told me; I had no tears left. Where had Colton been all these hours that he was supposed to be at practice, and who had he been with? I think we already knew the answer to that one. All we could do was wait for the next few hours for Colton to come home, but he did not come home.

We had begun to wonder if he had found out about Joe and Mandy going to the game and had run away again. With that in mind we went up to the loft to see if we could find any information to tell us what was going on. I opened his science book only to find sexually explicit pictures of Desiree and notes from her indicating Colton and she had begun a sexual relationship while he was staying at her home. Desiree's parents had even allowed them to sleep in the same bed. The letters also indicated they had never broken up; it was only a game, and they were still very much sexually active.

Marissa acted extremely agitated and upset during this time, assuring us Colton would not run away again. She said all this even as he was becoming increasingly late.

I asked her, "Marissa, how could you not know? You were at school with them every day. You said Desiree was crying; you said they had broken up. You said he was at football practice. You were lying all this time."

"No, Mom, I promise. He must have been lying to me. I didn't know."

Finally Colton walked in the door and said, "Man, I am so tired. We did not play well so the coach made us stay after and run laps for the next hour. I'm wiped out."

"What was the score?" Joe asked.

"I don't know the final. It just got way out of hand. We were way behind, and that's why the coach got so mad," he answered.

"Colton, your dad and Amanda were at the game. You are not even on the team. Where have you been?" I asked.

There was no answer. He certainly was not going to tell us anything because he had no idea what we knew and what we did not.

I was so tired. I just wanted my family back, and I did not want to have to deal with this anymore. I still could not understand what had happened. We once had the perfect family, but now, more and more, that family was just an illusion.

Colton finally admitted he had never joined the football team; it was all a ploy so he could spend more time with Desiree. He had never broken up with her; he never had any intention of doing so. He was going to her house daily, spending time with her and her parents. These were the same parents we had demanded have no contact with him and the same parents who had once lied to us and then laughed at our pain.

Equally hard to accept was finding out Marissa had been party to it all along. She helped Colton make up his lies, and he helped her. We had once believed in the "buddy system." We were sure the children were safer and more honest if they had someone with them to hold them accountable. Colton and Marissa had used this concept to create a cover for all their actions. Each told us exactly what they thought we wanted to hear, and each had the promise and "the dirt," if you will, on the other to assure complete secrecy.

There had not been one moment of truth in all the weeks since they returned. Every emotion, every feeling, every conversation had been based on deceit. It was becoming increasingly clear these two children had no conscience. There was nothing they were not capable of, no boundary they would not cross and no remorse for those who got hurt along the way.

Chapter Eleven

Betrayed Again

It was difficult to continue the hard work of clearing and cleaning the verandah. Yet there was so much work left to be done. It seemed with each passing memory I was finding less and less will to continue. I had already accomplished so much today; I had to fight the urge to give up and say "good enough." I knew in my heart that it was not "good enough." The flowers and bushes that so wanted to survive were still being strangled by the weeds that were trying to take over. I knew I had to cut them away for the other plants to have any chance of survival. The weeds were no different from the lies in our lives, and until we could find truth again, we would continue to be strangled by them.

We had no idea what to do next. It was obvious we were in so far over our heads. Joe and I both wanted nothing more than for Colton and Marissa to succeed; we just had no idea how to get there. On a daily basis we spent hours counseling them. We tried to make our expectations and consequences clear, and more than anything we tried to show them how much we loved them and forgave them. We forgave even though we still did not understand.

Some days I believed we were making progress—progress from what, I was not sure. Prior to that day, only weeks before, I had believed we were a family full of love and mutual respect. Now I had no idea what each person's role was. I was beginning to question what was real and what was not. Mostly I questioned if Marissa or Colton ever loved us, or if it was all just a game and we just didn't know we were playing.

It was Friday. The kids were excited about the upcoming week since it was fall break. I had made an agreement with each of them that if they brought their midterm grades home, prior to the holiday, and the grades were acceptable, they would not have to do any homework over the break. Each of them, except Colton and Marissa, did just that. They both had "inadvertently" left their grades at school. I told them they would have to do the two hours of homework each day that had been promised them. As they sat at the kitchen table to begin their homework, the phone rang. It was a recorded message from the school informing us that both of them had missed one or more classes of school that day.

They vehemently denied this was true, and I was in a difficult position to argue since the school was closed and I had no way of verifying they had actually missed. I knew I would not be able to act on this until the following week so I dismissed it and instead concentrated on their doing their schoolwork. I wrote a contract with each of them listing the expectations we had of them over the break, and each agreed without opposition. They completed their homework that night and then had some free time before bed.

About 10:00 I went up to my bedroom. Joe was in the theater watching a movie, and the other kids were downstairs. As I went into my room I noticed Marissa's light on; I went in to say good night. She was in the Jack-n-Jill bathroom that separated her room from Amanda's, but she was not alone; Colton was in the bathroom with her. They were standing at the double sinks in front of the mirror and appeared to be whispering.

As a mother, I instantly knew something was wrong. It is hard to describe that feeling, but it is overwhelming. I talked to them for a few moments, just pleasantries, when I noticed my heart had begun to race. I sensed there was a secret, and I was afraid.

As I walked out of the bathroom into Marissa's room, my eye caught her backpack on the floor; it appeared to be stuffed with something. I picked it up and unzipped it. It was full of her clothes, her makeup, her curling iron, her jewelry, all the things she valued. I sat down on the floor next to it. There was no denying; they were leaving again. I was drained, emotionally and physically. I did not feel I even had the energy to confront them, but I would need to find it.

As Marissa walked in from the bathroom, I asked, "Marissa, you are leaving again?"

She sat down on the bed. "Well, Colton and I are thinking about leaving tonight," she answered impassively.

"Colton," I called out—sure that when he answered he would tell me none of this was true. After all, he had promised me he would never leave again, especially not in the middle of the night. He promised that if he ever left he would leave through the front door. I knew this could not be true; at least I prayed it could not.

Colton then came in and sat on the bed with Marissa. "Colton, are you going to leave again?" I asked.

"Yea, we were thinking about it."

"But you promised. How could you do that? Why would you do it?"

There was no answer, no comfort or relief. They were quiet, and their eyes showed no emotion. For the first time I was forced to accept that my words had no power. I could not ask a question; they would simply lie to me. I could not give advice or offer guidance; they no longer looked to me for that. I was powerless in this situation.

Still I begged Marissa not to go. I reminded her she would be eighteen in only a couple of months, and then Joe and I would help her get her own apartment. She was already enrolled in college classes. I assured her she did not need to run; she was almost on her own. I begged her to let us help, all to no avail. Finally I asked her where she would live. She said she would live on the streets and sleep in a ditch; it did not matter to her. I could not understand where the hatred had come from. Only an hour before she had hugged me and told me how much she loved me and how much she appreciated my support; now she looked at me with a soulless stare.

Colton just looked down from where he was sitting toward the floor. I had not noticed it at first, but in the midst of Marissa's clothing were several spiral notebooks. I knew Marissa liked to keep spirals to send notes back and forth to her friends at school. I picked up the first notebook, and finally I saw emotion in their faces; unfortunately it was anger.

I began to read. I read each note aloud, and with each note both of them became increasingly agitated. The notes explained how Desiree and Colton were still seeing each other, how they would skip classes and meet at her house, and how they had found ways to fool the attendance office. They went on to describe, in detail, sexual encounters between Colton and Desiree and the depth of their relationship. It was obvious from the notes that Colton was sneaking out in the middle of the night to see her and then sleeping through his classes at school the following day. The notes further described their life of lies and deceit.

Marissa was proud of the lies she had told on Colton's behalf and how naïve we were to believe them. The letters mocked us and mocked our forgiveness and our misguided belief in them. They were cruel, heartless and evil. As I read each one, I began to feel that these were two strangers sitting before me. I did not know them. They had lived a dual life, one that used people, stole things, manipulated, swindled and conned to obtain anything and everything they wanted.

It had taken me a long time to accept this because I believed in them; I truly believed every lie. I had assisted them in this deception because I wanted so much for their lies to be truth. They took my faith, my trust and my love and traded them for this other life. I thought about going down the stairs and getting Joe, but I guess my first instinct was to try to spare him the incredible grief I now felt. It would be unbearable to share that pain with someone I loved; I did not know what to do.

After a few moments I stood. I looked at my children, not knowing if I would ever see them again and quietly said, "If you are going to leave, then leave now. You will not leave this family again in the middle of the night for us to wonder where you are. You will walk out the front door just as you promised."

Neither one of them stood. It was one thing for them to make the decision to leave, but they were not going to let me make that decision for them. Again I told them to get their shoes; they were going to leave. They continued to sit. My voice became stern, and with that they finally stood. Colton pushed past me, hurried out of the room and started gathering his things. He picked up his backpack and started stuffing it with everything he could get his hands on. I was so angry and hurt; I guess I thought that if he did not have any of his things he would not leave. I reached out and took the backpack from him. He was so much stronger; he grabbed it from me, and as he did he flung me against the bunk bed. We struggled for a few more minutes until I finally conceded that he was going to leave, with or without his things. It was over.

I stepped back, and he started toward the stairs. Marissa ran from her room and cut in front of him so she headed down the stairs first. Colton was directly after her. I was still behind them, sure that at any moment they would decide they did not want to go. They continued to head for the front door; I stopped on the stairs. The door was locked, and I watched as they fumbled to get it open and finally ran out. Colton slammed the storm door so hard that it shook the front of the house.

His last words to me, his mother for the past ten years, the one he vowed his love to each day, the one who held him when he was sad, comforted him when he was sick and always, always adored him, were ones of profanity.

I stood on the stairs and watched through the window as they hurriedly walked down the street. They had an angry stride, and it was evident Colton was still yelling. He was carrying his bag as if he was proud he had taken one last thing from us.

I took a breath and then sat down on the stairs for a few moments; I knew they would never be back. I felt God's presence, and in the silence, He spoke that to me. The wound was deep; no one who has not experienced the loss of a child can understand the depth. Still I had to compose myself; I had to tell Joe what had just happened.

I walked into the theater. He must have been able to tell from the look on my face that something was desperately wrong. He immediately reached for the remote and turned the movie off. I sat down in the chair next to him and quietly said, "They are gone."

I remember the look on his face. "What?" he asked more than once. "What do you mean?"

I then had the arduous task of telling him what had transpired. I felt for a moment his judgment of wondering if I couldn't have done something to prevent this, or if I had come and gotten him, if he couldn't have done something. I was not sure if the judgment was his or if it was mine. He was so hurt, and I felt he was disappointed in me. I showed him the letters; he read them, just as I had, losing a little bit of his heart with each one.

When he had finished he said, "You did the right thing. I wish I had been there with you, but it is probably better I was not. With Colton that angry and with me wanting to protect you, well, it is probably better I was not."

Still, I was sad for him. It was two of his children, as well as mine, that had walked out that door; yet only earlier that evening they had been joking and laughing together. Now he had not even been given the opportunity to say good-bye.

Together we had to tell the other children. They had been through so much over the past two months; I did not think they could possibly bear anymore. Johnny and Willy had been asleep on the bunk beds in the loft. Through all the confusion I had forgotten they were there. They had pretended they were asleep, but both of them told us they had seen and heard everything. They offered the story to the other children. I allowed each of the older children to read the spirals; I needed them to know I had not just thrown Marissa and Colton out.

I thought they would be very upset. If they were, they hid their emotions. Each acted as if it had no impact of them. They were tired of the drama, and they missed the life they once knew. I wanted so much to give that back to them, but I could not. That life was lost.

We did not hear anything that weekend. We made a decision not to call the police until Monday morning. We had already had so much police involvement, and they acted so slowly on the last runaway report that we did not feel any rush.

On Monday morning Joe called the sheriff to report them missing again. It was odd because, as he was talking to them on the phone, the doorbell rang, and it was a sheriff. I was confused because there was no way he could have possibly gotten to our house that soon.

"Are you Deborah Hannah?" he asked.

"Yes, what is this about?" I answered.

"We have a report of child abuse and neglect against you that we are investigating."

"What?"

"Colton and Marissa Hannah contacted our office this morning and filed a police report stating they had been physically abused by you and that you had thrown them out of the house on Friday night."

"No, they ran away. I mean, they were going to run away, but I found out and told them to leave. We are calling the runaway report in right now," I clarified.

Then, as if in my defense, I said, "Have you seen Colton? He is over six feet tall and weighs almost 170 pounds. There is no way I could abuse him."

"Well, why didn't you report it Friday night if they ran away?"

I tried to explain to him that when Marissa and Colton ran away the last time, no officer got back with us for days, and so we did not feel it was imperative to call immediately. He seemed disinterested, and it was evident he was more interested in looking around the house and talking with the other children. He was at our house for a short time and then said he was going over to see Colton and Marissa and take a full report.

"You know where they are?" I asked.

"Sure. They found a friend to take them in," he answered. With that, he left assuring us he would be back.

When he left, Joe and I sat down on the couch. He reached out to hold my hand and reminded me of a Bible verse he used to quote to me years ago when I was afraid. It was from 2 Timothy 1:7. "For God has not given us a spirit of timidity, but a spirit of power, of love and of self-discipline." He tried to comfort me. We tried to comfort each other, but we knew the worst was yet to come. Within an hour we were contacted again by Social Services and informed that allegations of abuse and neglect had been made against us, me specifically, and since this was our second report a full investigation was warranted. She then told me we needed to have our children available at 3:00 p.m. that day or the county department would go to their school. The caseworker who had once treated me with respect and kindness was now stern and suspicious.

About an hour later the sheriff arrived back. He said that based on Colton and Marissa's allegations he had made the decision to turn it over to the authority of Social Services. He said that since neither of the children had any injuries or markings of previous injuries he had decided not to follow through with this on a criminal level. He assured us that charges of abuse and neglect were likely to come, but it would be through Social Services not through the sheriff's department.

I suppose we were slightly relieved we were not going to be arrested, but the doubt and uncertainty of what lay ahead frightened us. We did exactly what we were told by Social Services. We called each of the children and had them leave whatever they were doing. Amanda was at work, Joey at football practice, Paul and Will at a friend's house, and Amy and Johnny still in school. We rounded everyone up, sat down as a family and explained what was going to happen next.

"A caseworker is going to come to the house, much like last time, and ask you exactly what happened with Colton and Marissa; all you have to do is tell the truth. You have nothing to be ashamed of and nothing to hide. Just tell the truth," Joe told them.

About that time the caseworker arrived. She informed us she would interview each member of the family separately in a different room and the investigation would take several days. She asked to be taken around the entire house and shown where children slept and where their belongings were. When she finished she called the first child into the office. It was Amanda's turn.

I cannot explain what it feels like to sit on the couch in the family room knowing your child is being interviewed in the other room and the woman conducting the interview has the power to take that child from you. I felt so ill from the anxiety and helplessness that had become my life.

Each of the kids went in for what seemed like an eternity and returned with grim and solemn faces. Everyone, that is, except Amy—she came out almost proud of herself. "I put that woman in her place," she said. "The caseworker asked me if I was ever being abused or if you were ever being mean to me, who would I go to? Who would I tell? I guess she wanted to know I had support. I told her, "I would tell my mom."

She said, "No, you don't understand. Who would you tell if your mom was the one abusing you?"

Amy said, "No, you don't understand. I would tell my mom. I would tell her I did not think she was being fair, and she and I would talk about it and come to a compromise. I would have nothing to tell anyone else." Then she sat down beside me, held my hand and said, "Don't worry, Mom. No one is going to believe any of this."

When the caseworker finished for the day, she talked to us for a few minutes and then assured us she would be back the following morning. We would again need to have the children at home; this was not over yet. I tried to be strong. I knew the children were looking to me as to the seriousness of this. I also understood Joe needed to know he did not have to worry about me along with everything else; I wish I had been that strong.

The following morning I sat down with the caseworker alone. "I know you have heard horrible stories about me," I said, "but here are some of the poems and letters Colton and Marissa have written me over the years. They are about how much they love me and our home and how blessed they felt by being adopted by our family."

I showed her the contract Colton and I had completed. "If I was going to beat him," I said, "why would I have drawn up a written contract with him stating exactly what the consequences of his not fulfilling it would be?"

I handed the letters and poems to her, and as she read them, I began to sob. I had cried so many tears in the last months that I was surprised I had any tears left. "Listen," I said. "I was not a perfect mother by any means, but I loved my children, and each and every day of my life I made a conscious effort to show them just that. I cannot defend myself against something I did not do. You have to tell me what they allege. I still may not be able to prove my innocence. I don't even know how to do that, but at least I will have a chance."

"Well," she answered, "one allegation is that you beat Johnny so severely you had to keep him home from school for four days, for the bruises to heal, so you would not be found out."

"Amy," I called out. "Will you please go to Johnny's school and have them print out an attendance record for this year and last? I need it right away."

"No problem," she said as she left.

I was not sure how much Johnny had missed, but I was certain he had never missed four days in a row. I looked back at the caseworker. "What else do they claim?"

"They were vague. There were not many actual incidents of abuse claimed but an overall assertion that they had been abused, but even more so that Willy and Johnny had been abused."

"How do I defend myself against that?" I asked.

She made no reply but instead continued her interviews with family members and her investigation.

Within the hour Amy arrived back. She asked to speak to me on the front porch, and I was sure the news was bad, that Johnny had indeed missed four days of school.

"Mom," she said smiling, "Johnny was not absent one day all last year or this. He was tardy five times for either doctor or orthodontist appointments, but he was never absent."

I should have jumped up and down with joy; instead I sat down on the rocking chair and stared at the paper. How had I reached the point in my life where I needed verification for each statement I made, and what would happen if I could not find that proof? My word was no longer enough. To the world I was capable of any act, no matter how disturbing. This paper was somehow more important than the years of my life I had devoted to Marissa and Colton, to nurturing and caring for them, to loving them and believing in them unconditionally. Their words against me trumped any actions on my part. I thought of the quote by Alexander Pope. "At every word, a reputation dies."

The investigation continued for several more days, but I sensed the mood of it changing. The investigation finally concluded with the statement "no foundation for the claims made." There was no statement of innocence; but then again innocence had been lost a long time ago. Still we needed to be thankful it was finally over.

In the end, how incredibly naïve of us to have believed that was true; it was by far not over...

That afternoon the caseworker came back to the house and sat down with us. "Colton and Marissa are both under the age of eighteen," she began. "Marissa has about eight weeks left until her birthday, but that is of little consequence.

In the state of Colorado you can be held liable for much longer. We can be involved until she can be fully emancipated. We will have to teach her how to get a job, a bank account, transportation and a place to live before we can step out of this."

"Are you serious?" I asked. "She already had all those things. She was enrolled in college, she had a job, and she had a checking and a savings account. She had a driver's license, and we had even bought her a car. She had a cell phone, and most of all she had a safe and loving place to live. She chose to give all that up, and yet we are responsible until you 'teach' her how to do the things she already knows how to do?" Exasperated I added, "Are you kidding?"

Her answer was short. "It's the law. Oh, and by the way you are still financially responsible for her, and since she still has braces on we of course will need you to continue paying for those."

"Now, if there are no more questions," she went on to say, "we need to figure out where to go from here. We can place them back in your home, but the truth is they will just run away again, so we need another option. The woman whose house they are staying at has agreed to keep them if you will allow that."

I could not believe my ears. Joe and I had raised these children for the past ten years; yet a woman they knew less than a week was now offering to let them stay there, and that was what they wanted. "Who is this lady?" I asked.

"When Colton and Marissa ran away they stayed at Desiree's house for the first couple of days, but when her parents said they needed to leave they moved into the neighbor's house. These neighbors are good friends with Desiree's family and, considering the charges of abuse against your family, feel like Colton and Marissa really need their help. They want to protect them from you and give the children a chance to succeed."

"Give the children a chance to succeed?" I asked. "They were loved and adored here. They had every opportunity to succeed." Suddenly I felt as if I were living in a parallel universe where nothing made sense.

"Do they know the claims made against us were false?" I asked.

"We do not discuss the investigation with anyone other than the direct parties involved. They know of the claims, and they know we have been investigating. It does not matter if the claims were false or not; the children do not want to come home. We have to make alternative arrangements. We can take them into Social Service custody, but you will be charged with neglect because they are minors and should be at home—or we can try to work this out."

"What are you asking us to do?" Joe interrupted.

"I am asking you to come to some kind of agreement with her and her husband to have the children stay there. They can continue to attend school and be with their friends. It would be the best thing for them."

Joe and I just put our heads down. "Are you asking us to relinquish our parental rights?" Joe asked.

"No, I need to be very clear about this. Both of you will still be completely liable civilly and financially; that will not change. You will just not have physical custody or authority in their day to day lives."

"Let me try to understand this." I sighed. "You are asking us to have no parental decision-making ability but still be responsible for whatever they might do."

"I know that doesn't sound good, but it is the best we can do with the situation we have at hand," she continued.

"What is this woman's name?" Joe asked.

"Roseanne Dempster."

Roseanne Dempster. I was not sure why that name sounded so familiar. I was sure I knew it, but I could not place it. The conversation was continuing between Joe and the caseworker, but I was no longer hearing them. I was still trying to figure out who this person was.

Finally I had it. "Joe, that's the woman from the football game."

"What?" he asked.

"Remember the football game a couple of weeks ago? Remember that woman who was so out of control? That's her."

"Oh, no," was his only response.

About three weeks prior, the whole family attended the Friday night football game at the high school. Joey was starting as varsity receiver, and we were looking forward to some quality family time. After about the first quarter I glanced over a few rows from us and saw Desiree sitting with her friends. I was surprised by this since supposedly Colton and Desiree no longer had any contact. If that were true, she would have no reason to be at this game; it was not her school, and she was not friends with anyone who went there.

I questioned Colton, who was sitting next to me, about it. He assured me he had no idea why she was there, but it had nothing to do with him. Still I watched, and it was becoming evident there was eye contact between them. I knew there was more to this story.

About that time a woman came storming up into the stands and began screaming at me. I had no idea who she was and had trouble even making sense of what she was saying. I did get that she was angry with Marissa and Amy for something she thought they had said to her daughter. She continued to yell for a few more minutes and then walked away.

I looked at Amy and asked, "What is she saying?"

Marissa interrupted. "She's the mother of Desiree's friend, Brittany. Desiree and Brittany are so mad at you because you will not let Desiree see Colton anymore that they are just making this up. We promise we did not do that."

I passed the keys over to Amanda. "Take the girls home. I don't want them to be here if this woman comes back."

Marissa jumped in. "No, Mom, I don't want to leave you here. I'll stay with you. I don't want anything to happen to you. I'm not going to go. I'll be with you."

"No, Marissa, it is not safe. Go home now with Amanda," I hurriedly repeated as I picked up their coats and belongings to leave. They left, all the while looking back to see what was going to happen next.

I was relieved they were gone, but as I looked to Colton for answers a man came bolting up the stairs. He began precisely where this woman had left off. We found out later it was her brother. He began screaming profanity, calling me names and threatening all kinds of things. It had become a very uncomfortable situation for everybody around us. They were trying to watch a football game, and now we were all in the middle of quite the drama.

Joe took my hand and quietly said, "Don't say anything to this man."

Just then a friend of our family, Mark, stood up and said, "You need to back off and leave her alone."

"What are you going to do about it?" the man responded.

With that, he pushed Mark. Mark pushed back, and before I knew it there was a brawl in the stands and the police were pulling both men off each other. The police escorted both of them out of the game, and we were left sitting on the bleachers with everyone staring at us. We were not even sure what had just happened.

Just then Colton put his arm around me and said quietly, "I am so glad someone finally did something because I was getting ready to punch the guy myself. I was seriously going to hurt him if he didn't stop."

I remembered it all, and now it finally made sense. "Joe, don't you see they set us up? Marissa was involved. She didn't want to leave because she was having fun watching what she had created, not because she wanted to stay with me. Colton was not going to protect me; he orchestrated this. Mark put himself on the line to defend me against something my own children had wanted to happen."

"There is no way we can work with this woman," Joe stated firmly.

"Yes, I knew there was some bad blood between your families, but that doesn't change what we need to do here," the caseworker continued.

"No, there is not bad blood between us. We do not even know them," I said.

"Whatever happened is of little consequence. What are you going to do now?" she asked again.

"I don't get it. This woman was so angry at Marissa at the game, and now she wants to raise her; there is something more here. Does she know who we are?" I asked.

"Yes, she knows exactly who you are and thinks it would be in the children's best interest for them to remain with her. Colton and Marissa both want to stay. My suggestion is that you draw up some kind of agreement and have everyone sign it, and then we can let the kids stay there."

This was impossible to comprehend; it was one more betrayal by the children we loved. That whole night at the football game—they had done that to us. What else would they do if they did not get their way? Yet, as impossible as it is to believe, I still worried about them. I did not want them to go into Social Service custody if it could be prevented, and it was clear Social Services was going to fight us if we did make that decision. We had no choice; we had to meet with these people.

Roseanne called later that day to arrange a meeting. She did what most people do when they still want to deceive and manipulate you with the intention of getting exactly what they want. She apologized for her behavior at the game and said she had been misinformed. I neither accepted nor rejected her motion. I said nothing except agreed to meet that evening at 7:00.

I then drew up a custody agreement in which Joe and I agreed to pay them eight hundred dollars a month, a figure they came up with, to support Colton and Marissa. In return we required that both children attend school, maintain a C average, have no trouble with the law, not be involved with alcohol or drugs, and abide by a curfew. Failure to abide by these rules would result in their being placed in the custody of the county. Joe and I looked it over repeatedly before they came. Neither of us could imagine how we had gotten here.

They arrived right on time. This woman who had verbally attacked me only weeks earlier was now sitting casually in my home, and I was signing my children over to her. She looked around, and I sensed she was surprised by what she saw. I am sure the stories Colton and Marissa had told her did not jive with what she was seeing. I do not know what she expected us to be like, but she genuinely seemed taken aback. We did not have much conversation. Each of us looked over the papers and signed.

Then Roseanne said, "My husband was homeless and had no one in his life who cared for him. He too came from an abusive home. A lovely family came along and took him in, and he ended up a great success. He truly was the "Homeless to Harvard" story. We plan to do the same thing in these kids' lives. We will give them what they have never had."

I could not breathe; I just could not breathe. How dare she say such a thing? These children did not come from an abusive home, they had everything, and mostly they had our undying love. I wanted to speak, but I did not have it in me to continue to defend my family or myself. To everyone we had become the people of Marissa and Colton's distorted fantasy; nothing I could say would change that. I had to give up the idea that our loving, supportive and respectful family ever even existed.

Just when I thought she could say nothing worse, she did. She happily chimed in, "They have taken to us so quickly. Marissa even asked after only three days if she could start calling us Mom and Dad. That made us feel so good."

That felt like a knife through my heart. I was their mother; Joe was their father. We had stayed up with them at night when they were scared. We had met all their needs, did their homework with them, had long conversations with them about life, and told them daily how much they were treasured. We had traded our lives to give them opportunity. We had invested ten years of our hearts and souls, and it meant nothing for these people had earned the same title in only three days.

I had thought I was broken before that day. I had no idea what true brokenness felt like until that moment. I stood up and handed them their coats, and as I shut the door behind them, I slid down the wall to the floor. I put my face in my hands and wept uncontrollably. Joe sat down on the floor next to me and put his arm around me. He did not say anything; there was nothing to say.

In the words of Johann Wolfgang Von Goethe, "Against criticism a man can neither protest nor defend himself; he must act in spite of it, and then it will gradually yield to him." We had no choice but to accept what had happened to us and we had to continue with our family in spite of it.

The accusations by Marissa were relentless; she continued alleging our abuse against Colton, Johnny and herself. Unfortunately, she added another troubling one; she claimed that she was sexually abused by Joey over the years. She told this disturbing story to anyone who would listen. I addressed this with her once in a letter, in her note I received in return, she wrote, "Joey is lucky he never did anything to me or I would have had him arrested." I held on to that letter hoping we would never have to use it but accepting that we may. She never did let the story die, but I knew that those who would believe such a claim would never be swayed by our possession of this letter. With that in mind, I high-lighted her lines, placed the letter in the drawer, and as we had become so accustomed to, we put our heads down and continued to take it.

Nevertheless, it is true that in life, more often than not, we get exactly what we ask for; this was no exception for Roseanne. Over the next days and weeks, Roseanne besieged us with phone calls. She was upset because as soon as the papers had been signed Colton and Marissa began skipping school, not keeping their curfew or, for that matter, following any of her rules. She feared they were beginning to have a negative impact on her own children. I remember once she called and screamed, "You are their mother! This is your responsibility. You need to do something."

I could do nothing; I had not seen or talked with either of my children since the night they left. I had lost my children. They had betrayed every moment we shared together, and now I was trying to problem-solve with a woman who was addicted to anger and conflict. On top of that, Social Service did not return my phone calls since the matter in their eyes had been resolved.

The phone calls became relentless, and the instability I had first witnessed in Roseanne began rearing its ugly head. Finally the caseworker became involved. She called me because she was upset that Roseanne was calling her on a daily basis. One day she would want to take us to court to revoke our parental rights because she wanted to adopt the kids, and the next day she wanted them removed from her home. She even went as far as to tell the caseworker we had lied and tried to deceive her about the behavior of Colton and Marissa to sucker her and her husband into taking them. It would have been comical if only it had not been so tragic.

This period of instability lasted two months. I am sure Colton and Marissa fueled the fire by making grand promises of doing everything that was required of them; they were charming and believable. I am sure Roseanne fell into the same place where we had been; she believed them. I am equally sure that belief quickly turned to anger when the deceptions were revealed.

I will be honest. Even though I made every effort to accommodate this woman, the truth is I had neither respect nor empathy for her. Still I did worry about her family; her volatility was mounting. I even began to wonder if Colton and Marissa were safe there. Then reality set in. Colton and Marissa cared only for themselves; they were far too narcissistic and self-serving to allow anyone to hurt them.

Colton continued to see Desiree through this time; Roseanne did not see it as a destructive relationship. Marissa became involved with a man she met. I did not know exactly who he was, but I knew his name to be Malachi, which made me believe he was the same boy she had been involved with years earlier before I decided to home school her. Regardless of whom they were involved with, neither was about to let anyone including Roseanne Dempster, dictate rules or expectations to them.

This angered Roseanne, and when our family left town for the Thanksgiving holiday she exploded. Since she could not make her many daily phone calls to us complaining of their behavior and since Social Services was not available, she was left without an outlet for her frustration. When we returned we knew the kids' time there was ending. Colton and Marissa had threatened to run to California with Desiree. Desiree's biological father still lived in California, and this had recently become inviting to all of them.

Roseanne called on the day we returned and said, "I want these kids out of here by 5:00 p.m. today. No ifs, ands or buts. I want them gone."

When I told her I had no authority to do that, she called Social Services. The caseworker was also out of town for the holiday so she asked to speak with her supervisor. Roseanne then informed this supervisor that Colton and Marissa needed to be removed by 5:00 p.m. that day.

Social Services filed the papers to remove both Colton and Marissa on December 4, 2003, and subsequently charged Joe and me with neglect of minor children because they were no longer living in our home and the county deemed them delinquent. The court hearing was set for the following Monday morning and we were advised to obtain legal counsel. The retainer was $3,000.00, but considering everything, it was not the biggest price we paid.

Days later, as we walked through the metal detectors into the county courthouse, we passed by an area that seemed so familiar. Then I remembered we had stopped there so many years ago to have our pictures taken only moments after the adoption. This was the same courthouse where it had all begun. It was the courthouse that was once filled with family and friends who shared our joy, our hope and our anticipation of the future. Now, all these years later, we walked in alone. We were now the accused, with no support or loving gestures from those who cared about us.

We had begun this journey blindly, but we had not noticed the darkness, in light of the love of those who supported us and our love for each other. In the absence of that, we became fully aware of the darkness, and in it we walked alone.

Colton appeared in court; Marissa went on the run. Roseanne was there and had brought several women with her for support. She had decided she did again want the children. She asked to speak with the judge; she was denied and was asked to leave the courtroom, along with those other women.

As expected, Joe and I were charged. We were given our rights and instructions from the judge, and Colton was taken into custody; a warrant was put out for Marissa. There was no foster or group home vacancy to put Colton in at the time, so he was sent to a shelter for runaway kids for two weeks until one opened up.

When we walked out of the courtroom back into the hallway, I overheard a conversation between Roseanne and the caseworker. Roseanne was explaining to her she had wanted the children all along and I was the one who had fed her lies and made her call and give the children back. She went on to say it was all a mistake and she wanted to bring the kids back home with her. She began talking about what a horrible and abusive mom I was and how much good she was doing for Colton and Marissa. As she finished her sentence she looked over and saw me. I continued to walk, but she knew I knew what she was doing.

When Joe and I returned from court, the phone was ringing. We have caller ID so I knew ahead of time that it was Roseanne. I thought about not answering it but then reconsidered. After all, for the last two months I had been forced to deal with her; now I could tell her exactly how I felt. I answered the phone with a polite "what do you need?"

"Deb, I am so sorry for everything."

I was not fooled; I was not sure what her game was, but I knew for sure she was playing one. Her efforts at manipulation and deception were transparent, and best of all I no longer had to deal with them. Our contract was null and void. We still possessed parental rights for both Colton and Marissa, and now our only adversary would be Social Services and Family Court. Roseanne was no longer involved in any capacity. I knew she would not view her role as such, but that was what it was.

Calmly I interrupted. "Roseanne, I need you to listen very carefully. Colton and Marissa are both in the custody of the county. You are not entitled to nor will you receive any more information about this case. I am asking you now not to call this phone number again. If you do, we will seek legal action against you. Once more, do not call this phone number again." With that, I hung up with the tentative optimism that we would never again hear from this woman.

Chapter Twelve

The Truth

I climbed the ladder to begin washing the large light fixtures that once illuminated the nights we spent on this verandah. As I touched one of them it fell apart in my hand. It was shattered; I am not even sure what was holding it together, maybe just the dust and dirt. It had been broken all along; I had not been able to see it, but that did not change its brokenness. That realization touched my spirit. Maybe there was still more brokenness within our family that we could not see. Until we had the time to look at each area and each person's individual needs, we would have no idea of the true damage our family had sustained. I needed, for all of our sakes, to dig deeper.

It was only days before Christmas now. We knew it was going to be difficult, our first Christmas without two of our children. We also knew we had to find our way through it for the children's sake. With that in mind, we arranged to go and visit Cain at the residential treatment center where he was staying. We thought it would be a nice drive up the mountains, and after we picked him up we could take all the kids bowling and out to eat. It could be a pleasant day for us all. I went to bed that night with a certain peace that as bad as it had been it was now going to get better.

The phone rang about 11:00 p.m., awakening me. Joe was still downstairs, so I answered the phone by the bed.

"I am watching you," a distorted voice mumbled.

"What?" I replied.

"I am watching you from the big blue van in front of the house. I am looking at your yellow house. You know I am here."

"Who is this?" I cautiously asked.

More mumbling followed, but I could not decipher what he was saying; it was as if he were using something to disguise his voice. Still there was such a threatening tone, and he seemed to be adding detail so I would know he was really outside my home. Quickly I hung up the phone. It rang again; I answered. It was more of the same. This continued for several more phone calls until I finally decided to unplug the phone in our bedroom. I tried to fall asleep, but I was frightened by what had been said. I lay awake for hours wondering if the phone was still ringing downstairs.

In the morning I plugged the phone back in and was so relieved when it did not ring. We showered, dressed and rounded up all the kids. As we were getting ready to walk out the door I grabbed my cell phone. There were several messages I needed to retrieve. I hesitantly punched in my code, afraid of what I might hear.

The only thing I could make out, through the profanity, were the words, "You will be dead by morning." Then the voice was overshadowed by sexual sounds, ones I was afraid to listen too closely to. I suppose I had some sense then that it could be Colton, and the idea that it was him and the call was sexual in nature was more than I could bear. Then the sexual innuendos turned violent, and I had heard enough.

I erased the rest of the phone calls without even listening to them. I put my phone in my purse and tried to pretend nothing had happened. Our special day was overshadowed by the questions in my head of who would want to hurt me and why. I did not tell Joe the extent of the phone calls at this time. We actually did not have any time alone to talk because we were with the kids for the day. On the way home from the mountains, with the children asleep in the back, I had to tell him. We decided we would call the sheriff's department as soon as we got home.

The phone was ringing as we walked in the door. We decided not to answer it and see if whoever it was would leave a message. To our surprise he did. He left a threatening, disgusting message, directed toward me. In that message, as in the others, he described in detail what he would like to do to me. We had to distract the other kids so they would not hear what was being left on our answering machine. The ringing did not stop; neither did the messages. The caller seemed to be getting more and more pleasure out of each call.

Within minutes my cell phone began to ring again; I hurriedly shut it off. I went in the other room and called the phone company. "I want my number disconnected," I said. "I need it done right away." Within moments my cell phone no longer rang. As I was talking with the phone representative about changing my cell phone number, Joe's cell phone began to ring.

I was trying to hold it together, but I was becoming frightened. Joe went in to the office and called the sheriff. "We need somebody out here right now," he said. To our surprise within fifteen minutes the doorbell rang. Joe answered the door, and two officers entered. We asked the kids to go in the other room, but it was evident they were staying close.

Before Officer Roberts was able to make his way to the family room, the phone began ringing again. "Do you want me to get that?" he asked. I nodded my head. He picked up the phone and merely listened. Each time one call ended, another came in. After approximately seven or eight calls, the officer decided to identify himself in an effort to stop the harassment. Unfortunately this made no difference. The caller did not believe him, and so the calls continued.

The deputy who had accompanied the responding officer asked if Officer Roberts wanted to try to trace the calls. I interrupted that Joe and I had already contacted the phone company and they were tracing the calls, but it would take some time. They decided they wanted to go a different route.

After calling dispatch and explaining the situation, they were told to keep talking to the perpetrator while the number was searched. Within moments Officer Roberts received a transmission with the number from which the calls were being placed. It was traced to a phone that was registered to Brenda Sanford. She was the mother of Desiree Connor, Colton's girlfriend. Then Officer Roberts verified the number by calling it while the other officer was still on the phone with the caller. Sure enough he heard the beep. The caller answered, and Officer Roberts said, "Gotcha." The caller quickly hung up.

The officers left within a few moments saying they were going to Desiree's house and would call us as soon as they knew anything. A few hours later we received a phone call from Officer Roberts. He and his partner had gone to Desiree's house and as a side note arrested her stepfather for drunken and disorderly conduct. The main reason for his call was that Desiree admitted she had given her phone to Colton to use. She and Colton were not to have any contact, by court order, so she had secretly given him the phone to communicate with her. The police then contacted Colton at the foster home he was staying in and after a lengthy conversation were able to obtain a confession from him. They were now in the process of charging him with harassment and stalking.

My emotions were mixed. I wanted to know who was making the phone calls and have them stopped. I still had trouble imagining, however, that my own son could say those things to me. I was overwhelmed with sadness. I thought back over the calls and everything that had been said in them. I listened to the recordings again, this time knowing it was Colton.

I could not understand exactly what it was I had wanted. Would it have been better if it had been a complete stranger who had wanted to rape and kill me? In the end I guess it would have been.

I was not sure how everyone else was feeling. I knew they were worried about me, but I did not know if they felt fear for themselves; no one wanted to talk about it. While we were driving the next day, Johnny was sitting in the back and asked, "Mom, are you okay?"

I answered, "I am okay."

Johnny then said, "Cause I know how you feel."

I remember thinking this was odd. I did not know how Johnny knew how I felt; maybe he was just being empathetic. That was really the last that was said of the phone calls. None of us wanted to remember them.

Christmas passed. We survived and even found our moments of joy amidst the sadness. A couple of days after Christmas, my friend Monet and her children were over at the house visiting. We were in the kitchen, which is located directly under the loft. Johnny was in the loft playing. Monet and I began talking about the problems I was experiencing with Johnny's behavior since she was still dealing with similar behavior by her adopted daughter, Venus. We were each expressing our frustration in not being able to administer to their needs.

Suddenly Johnny was on the stairs. He was crying—not crying as if he was merely upset, but more as if he was in pain. He was close to hysterical. I jumped up. "What's wrong? What happened?"

"I need to talk to you, Mom," Johnny cried.

"Come on down," I said.

"No, I have to talk to you alone. I can't talk to you until she leaves," he said.

"Johnny, it is just Monet. You can say anything in front of her. Come on down."

"No, no, she needs to leave." Johnny was sobbing.

I looked at Monet. She said, "Come on, girls. We're going to leave now."

Venus and Olivia got their shoes and headed for the front door. Monet whispered,

"Call me and tell me what is going on." I agreed.

I walked back into the family room and called Johnny down the stairs. He was still crying. Joe came into the family room and sat in the big easy chair. I sat on the edge of the couch, and Johnny sat down on the coffee table directly in front of me. I glanced to the side and saw my daughter Amy and my niece in the kitchen. They were leaning over the island that separated the kitchen from the family room because they were equally curious.

"OK, Johnny. What's wrong?" I asked.

"It's something real bad," he said.

I then put my hand out to him and laid it on his leg. "Johnny, no matter what it is you can tell us," I said.

He cried for several more minutes and then finally muttered through his tears, "Marissa has been having sex with me for five years."

I remember feeling as you do when you find out someone close to you has died. I could not breathe; I could not speak; no words would come out. I am sure it was only moments, but it seemed as if it took forever for me to answer. Then it came to me. His definition of sex must be different from mine; he was just a little boy. I remembered back to when Paul was about six years old and I was tucking him in bed and saying his prayers with him.

"How old do you have to be to sleep with a girl?" he asked.

Stunned, I replied, "Well, you need to be married, and you probably won't get married until you graduate from college, so it will be about the time you are twenty-two or so."

"Man, I don't want to wait that long," Paul replied.

My voice began to crack, but I wanted to be approachable regarding all subjects. I knew I needed to be calm. So I cleared my throat and said, "Paul, it is perfectly normal that you are thinking about sex. I just didn't realize it would be so soon."

"Sex?" He seemed confused. "I don't want to have sex. I'm just tired of sleeping alone."

I laughed with such relief. I had learned my lesson. They speak as a child, but we hear them as adults. This must certainly be what was now going on with Johnny. I needed to be calm and let him explain to me what he meant by that statement.

"Johnny," I said softly, "everyone's definition of sex is a little different. I need to know what your definition is."

He cried a few more minutes. He seemed to be having a difficult time finding the words. Finally he put his head down, sniffled and said, "The regular way—I mean it the regular way."

The room seemed to close in. I saw nothing but his face. My heart was pounding so hard, and I was so scared. I could not understand what I was missing. What was he trying to say?

"Johnny, I don't know what the regular way is. I need you to tell me," I begged.

He seemed frustrated now, putting his head into his hands. He raised his voice and snapped, "I don't know what words to use."

I answered him with what he needed without even thinking. This was not real; it could not be. Any moment Johnny would tell me he had made a mistake and did not mean it this way.

With those words, he told us a disturbing account of long-term sexual abuse, graphic in detail, disgusting by nature, and horrifying in reality.

With that, Joe lurched forward in his chair, with a closed fist hit the top of the table and announced, "I knew it."

"Knew what?" I cried out.

He went on to say, "Deb, remember I saw them in the laundry room? It was several years ago. I walked past the laundry room to the theater and glanced over. I saw Marissa with Johnny and something did not look right. She jumped when she saw me.

"Remember? How could I remember that? I knew nothing about that," I answered in complete confusion. "What did you do?"

"I called Marissa into the theater first. I told her what I thought I saw. She laughed and assured me she was just helping Johnny snap his pants. She made me feel ridiculous for even asking. She had me question what I had seen. Why would a sixteen-year-old girl have any sexual feelings toward a seven-year-old boy? She was right; it made no sense. I told her she could leave, and then I asked Johnny to come into the theater.

I asked him if Marissa had ever touched him inappropriately. He acted shocked and convinced me she had never done anything like that to him. I asked him if he would be able to tell me or you if she ever did do anything. He guaranteed me he would.

I did not know what else to do; they were both denying it. Then I called you into the theater and told you about it. You said that was not possible and dismissed it."

"No, I would remember something like that," I said. "You didn't tell me."

"Dad," Johnny interrupted. "You're right. That is what happened. I had to lie to you because I was afraid of Marissa, and I was afraid of what Colton would do to me when Marissa told him what I had done. I'm sorry, Dad. I was just scared."

It was quiet for a few moments, and I finally realized that none of that mattered now. What mattered was the fact that Johnny was saying he had been abused by Marissa. I took a deep breath and tried to find clarity.

"Johnny, when did it start?" I said softly.

"I was in kindergarten or first grade." He was sobbing. "She touched me in the laundry room and asked me if I would tell. I said no, and so she kept doing it. She did it like a few times each week, and she kept doing more stuff each time."

"That was five years ago," I sadly sighed.

"When was the last time it happened?" Joe asked.

"It was when Bobby, the painter, was here to paint the inside of the house," Johnny replied. "Mom was home schooling Amy and Marissa. You, Mom and Amy had to go to the dentist, and Marissa was supposed to watch me. Bobby went to Taco Bell to get some tacos for his lunch, that is when Marissa did it.

"Can you tell us about any other times?" I asked.

"There are too many to say," he said, sobbing a little harder now.

"Johnny, please try," I begged.

"It happened when the big-screen TV was in the basement against that other wall. You were home schooling Marissa, and I was off track from my school. You had to go to the store, and Marissa was the one in charge. We went down in the basement and sat on the couch. She put in the movie 'Overboard,' and we got under the blanket, she made me have sex that day too," he continued.

"Johnny, how many times did it happen?" I asked again.

"Way too many for me to count. She did it all the time," he answered.

"Were Mom and I always gone from the house when it happened?" Joe asked.

"No, most of the time you were here. Marissa made me lie a whole bunch of times about what I was doing and what she was doing. You were usually here, just like in another room," he said.

My hands were shaking, and I glanced down at my shirt which was now wet with tears. I did not think I could go on with this conversation for another minute. I needed to get out of there. I knew I needed to comfort Johnny, but I was so torn. I had always told myself I would believe my child if he or she ever came to me claiming abuse. But this was different. If I believed Johnny, I would have to believe Marissa was a sexual perpetrator. It was too much to comprehend. I needed it not to be true—because if it was, what kind of mother had I been? How could this have happened in my house and I not have known it? I would have known; I felt that I would have.

I hugged Johnny; Joe did as well. We told him we were proud of him for having the courage to come forward and we would get him the help he so needed. I stood, trying to convey to him the conversation was over.

"Wait, Mom. There's something more!" he cried.

What more could there be? I thought. I was sure that if there was more I did not want to know it. I also knew I needed to. I sat back down. Johnny put his head down and wept. "Colton did it to me too," he said, sobbing.

"When? What happened?" I snapped. I was not angry with Johnny. I was angry at the situation in which I had so little control.

"It happened when we shared a room together when I was in third grade. I was on the top bunk, and Colton was on the bottom. He told me to come down on his bed; I did.

"How many times did it happen with Colton?" Joe inquired

"Just once, Dad. I promise, just once," Johnny said.

I did not feel good about that answer. Through our whole conversation this seemed to be the first time Johnny was holding back. I felt there was more so I asked, "Johnny, what would it mean if it happened more than once with Colton?"

"It would mean that I was gay."

Johnny had been able to speak in detail about what happened with Marissa, but he was having more difficulty speaking about Colton. This seemed to be a more painful memory for him. Now, he too wanted the conversation to be over. We comforted him for a few more minutes, and then he said how tired he was and he wanted to go to bed. We tucked him in.

I was happy he could sleep. I knew we would not be able to. I do not think we had yet completely processed what Johnny had told us. Along with Amy and my niece, we spoke briefly about what Johnny had said. We did not disbelieve what he had said; we were just afraid to believe it. We hugged good night and headed to our own rooms. Joe and I looked at each other in complete disbelief. Neither one of us knew what was real anymore. We had been through so much; how could we now survive this?

I lay in bed tossing, turning and staring at the ceiling. I had to get up once because I felt sick to my stomach. After a few hours of this I remembered something Johnny had said about Bobby painting the house and us going to the dentist. That fact could be proved or disproved; I hurried down the stairs to the filing cabinet in the office. Quickly I shuffled through the receipts of the contractors we had paid this year. We had paid Bobby on May 1st of this year. Now I just needed to look for the date of our previous dental appointment. I pulled out the copy, afraid to look. I gathered my courage and looked down; it was May 1st. I sat down on the office floor and wept as I never remember weeping before in my life. The pain was from such a deep place. I really believed I would not be able to survive this.

We had taken Johnny into our home to offer him an opportunity for a better life. I personally had promised his mother I would love and nurture him and would keep him safe; I had not kept that promise. The guilt and shame were unbearable. How could I have not known? I was devastated. That night seemed to never end; I do not think I ever slept. By morning it had become obvious we needed to call the sheriff's department. We had done that so many times over the past few months, but this was different.

I knew what we needed to do, but I did not know if we had the strength to follow through. To call the sheriff would be to make this public. Everyone would know what a terrible mother I had been. Everyone would know what I allowed to happen in my home. I was only beginning to let go of the fantasy that we had such a perfect family. Now I had to come to terms with the fact that it had all been a lie. There had not been honesty in our home for so many years; it was just my imagination. This time it was no one's fault but mine. Still, for Johnny to heal, I would need to tell. We could not keep this secret, no matter how tragic the consequence of telling it would be. Joe called the sheriff.

Sunday morning, within a half hour of when we called, the deputy arrived at our house. We invited him in, and he took the report. To our surprise he did not want to interview Johnny. He informed us that an investigator within the sexual abuse unit would contact us. With that, he left. We stumbled around the rest of the day trying to find some normalcy. Joey returned from his cousin's house, and we told him. Amanda came home, and we had to tell her. Paul and William, who had been home at the time Johnny disclosed this to us but were downstairs, also had to be told. I did not want to tell one more person. I wanted this shame to be our secret.

Unfortunately that was not possible. I had to call the caseworker assigned to Colton and Marissa. I had to tell her even if it meant she would have to open up yet another investigation; this was exactly what happened. This was our third Social Service investigation in so many months. While we were speaking with her, the investigator called us. He needed us to take Johnny to be interviewed on video tape and asked us to take him in the following day. He informed us we would not be allowed to be with Johnny during this interview, but he assured us that he and the caseworker would stay with him.

We did as we were told. Joe and I sat on the couch outside the interview room; a counselor sat with us for what seemed like an impossible amount of time. She tried to comfort us as well as offer some explanation as to how something like this could have happened. I heard her speak but not necessarily her words. My mind was in the adjacent room. At one point I remember even trying to hear what was being said. I, of course, could not. Finally they came out. The investigator sent Johnny off with a therapist to a separate room and then asked us to join him in the conference room. We sat down, and I looked at him and asked, "Do you believe him?" I was still trying to make this not true in my mind.

"Yes, he has incredible detail. I have been doing this for years. I absolutely believe him," the investigator responded.

I looked at Joe's face and could see his pain; it was the pain we both shared. I broke down. I laid my head on the table and wept yet again. I tried to stop but could not; I just wept.

The investigator began explaining to us what the next step would be in having Colton and Marissa charged. He informed us he would ask the district attorney to charge both Colton and Marissa with:

18-2-405.3(1),(2)(a) SEX ASSAULT/CHILD/POSTRUST-VICT UNDER 15

18-3-405(1),(2)(d) SEX ASSAULT/CHILD-PATTERN OF ABUSE

18-3-405(1) SEX ASSAULT/CHILD

He said we needed to focus our attention on two distinct areas, the therapeutic and the legal. We needed to be sure everyone's emotional needs were met at the same time as we were proceeding with legal action against both Colton and Marissa. This would be a difficult line to walk, he assured us. His words echoed as if in an empty room. I was hoping Joe was listening and comprehending what he was saying because I could not. Everyone stood, so I did as well. I was handed a card with the name of a therapist, and then Joe, Johnny—clutching his new teddy bear they had given to him—and I walked out to silently continue the journey through our nightmare.

Chapter Thirteen
Quest for Justice

~~~~~~

Titus 3:1
"Remind the people to be subject to rulers and authorities,
to be obedient, to be ready to do whatever is good,
to slander no one, to be peaceable and considerate,
And to show true humility toward all men."

~~~~~~

The truth had been revealed; now was the time for justice. The question remained: Justice for whom, for Johnny, for Colton and Marissa, for our family or our reputation? I thought justice meant righteousness, and righteousness encompassed virtue, honesty and integrity. How then would justice ever be applied to our lives?

I looked around me at the porch, nothing but the shattered ruins of our existence. How was this just? How could this ever be made right? How could we find justice for the accusations, the betrayal, the abandonment and the loss? We could not even make sense of any of it, and yet we needed to find justice.

As I felt the anger well up in me again, my eyes caught the simple wrought iron cross that hung by our front door. Underneath it the plaque read: "But as for me and my household, we will serve the Lord. Joshua 24:15." I found no comfort in this as I had before; instead it only made me angrier. We had served the Lord, we had done as we had promised, and our lives were still destroyed. I challenged God to show me the justice in any of it, in our isolation, our grief or even our sorrow.

I struggled to find the justice in our entire family being called down to the sheriff's department. I remembered that night so vividly. A cold, January evening, it had gotten dark so early, and the wind held such a bitterness. It seemed we were the only ones at the sheriff's department; it was quiet and eerie. Each of the children was taken to different rooms and questioned individually about what had transpired over the last years. They each wrote statements as to what they thought the truth was, none of them knowing what it really was.

Still that night was one of revelation, maybe not to the police, but to me. I was sitting in the open room, awaiting my turn, along with the caseworker. She looked at me and said, "Well, it all makes sense now."

"What makes sense?" I asked because it seemed to me nothing made sense.

"The allegations of abuse. They said you were abusing Johnny because they wanted us to remove him from your home before he had the chance to tell the truth. They discredited you so that if you ever did come forward, no one would believe you. They claimed abuse before you could."

In all this time, despite everything that happened, I had never spoken an ill word about either Marissa or Colton. I had always told the county, the sheriff, whoever was asking, that it must be a mistake; I never turned on them. Now I had to accept that they were willing to take everything from me, say anything about me, have me arrested, have my children taken from me—all if it benefited them. In their eyes I was not their mother; I was just expendable in their plan.

Fortunately I did not have the time to process this because Johnny came back out of the room and sat down next to me. The caseworker asked him if he remembered the day his dad saw him and Marissa together.

Johnny said, "Yes, you remember it too, Mom, don't you?"

"Johnny, I didn't know about that. Dad didn't tell me."

"Yes, Mom, he did. Remember it was a Sunday. We were all watching the football game. After Dad talked with Marissa and with me, he called you into the other room and told you. I was in there with you."

"Are you sure, Johnny? I don't remember."

"Yes, you told Dad it was not possible. You told him Marissa just loved me. She loved all children; she was a teenager, and I was just a little kid."

I don't know what it was about the way he said it, but suddenly I remembered. I remembered that day and Joe questioning me. I remembered thinking it was not possible.

I had separated the house. The girls had the second floor with Joe and me. They had their own bathrooms and sitting area. The boys had the basement with their own bathrooms and living room area. They even had separate laundry rooms. I was fully aware that sexual inappropriateness could become an issue, because we had so many children in the house that were not related. I watched certain relationships very carefully. I watched Marissa and Joey because they were close to the same age, Colton and Amy because they were the same age; but I had never thought to watch the relationship between a beautiful teenage girl and a little boy.

I had not been able to conceive it. I had not been able to envision it. And now Johnny had paid the price for my not being able to. Joe had told me, and I had so self-righteously proclaimed he did not. He had. He had seen the truth. I had convinced him the truth was a lie, when in fact the truth was those lies, all of them.

It took almost three months for the charges to be filed against Colton and Marissa. The lead investigator, Ken, filed the reports and then sent them to the district attorney. It is a slow process for the D.A. to decide whether to file charges and whether those charges are filed in the adult or juvenile courts.

During this three-month period the sheriff's deputies were at our house countless times. One morning we woke up, and Amy's car had been broken into. Her stereo had been stolen, and the inside of the car destroyed. Even her clothes were taken from the backseat. A few weeks later we woke up, and Joey's car had been broken into. His stereo was taken as well as all his paintball gear. He had worked an entire summer to purchase it, and yet it was gone in only a moment. A few weeks later we came out to find the tires had been slashed. Once our home was shot at with paintballs in the night. Each day brought the nervous anticipation of what else they could do to us. Eventually we had a security system installed in our home, on every window and every door. We had to face that we were no longer safe in our own home. Finally we went to court and asked that Colton be moved to another city for his foster care placement. There was much hesitation because there was no proof he was doing it; but as the incidents added up and his whereabouts were not able to be verified, the court finally decided to move him.

I wondered why we had not heard anything from Marissa. She was picked up in the back of a car making out with Malachi and placed in a juvenile treatment center, but she did not contact us. Yet we heard so much from Colton. I, in my never ending optimism, hoped the horrible things Colton was doing to us were only his way of trying to stay connected, like a small child seeking negative attention just so he could receive any of our attention. At the time it seemed a reasonable explanation.

We were involved in all the court proceedings and attended every hearing on the charges of juvenile delinquency, stalking, harassment, destruction of property, theft, vandalism and fraud; even though we knew we would never be able to find healing through this process. We knew, in our heads, that healing would have to come on an emotional level, but our hearts told us this would make us feel better. Our better judgment told us it would not, but still it was an attempt to reclaim some power in our lives. We wanted Marissa to be charged as an adult because the last time she abused Johnny she was only months away from her eighteenth birthday. She knew exactly what she was doing; she was no child, and we did not want her to be treated like one now.

We were less sure about Colton. From what Johnny had shared with us, Colton was only fourteen when he molested him. There were no other incidents, at least that Johnny would admit to, so we would accept that Colton should be charged as a juvenile and be subject to a much less severe consequence.

Joe called the investigator almost daily, waiting for the charges to be filed. Finally in March it happened. Joe called and Ken informed him that an arrest warrant had been issued for both Colton and Marissa. The D.A. had decided to prosecute both of them as juveniles. This was a tough blow, but Joe quickly pushed past it and went on to when the warrants would be served. Ken responded with, "These things take time."

For Joe, this was just not good enough; there had been too many acts of violence against our family. For our sakes, Joe needed Colton and Marissa to be off the streets. He decided to call the police department directly to give them the whereabouts of both of them; he needed them picked up that day. It was a Thursday afternoon, and a few hours later we received the call that Marissa was in custody. She had been taken to an adult facility since she was over the age of eighteen, and her arraignment would be in the morning. We were deeply discouraged that Colton had not been picked up. He was either not at the address we gave them, or he was hiding out.

The next day I received a phone call from Roseanne, the woman I had hoped never to hear from again. She asked me what was going on; several different police cars were surrounding Desiree's house, and one officer had his gun pulled. I briefly shared with her that Marissa had been arrested and Colton was next. She became hysterical and said she had let both Colton and Marissa baby-sit for her small children and I should have warned her of the kind of deviants they were. If it had not been for the fact that a real possibility existed that something could have happened to her children I would have been tempted to seek some pleasure in her distress. Nevertheless I could not; someone else's pain could not eradicate my own.

Colton was not at Desiree's house, as the police found when they entered the home. They decided to have a police car wait for him at his foster home when he returned. As he walked up they grabbed him, put his head down on the hood of the car, cuffed his hands behind his back, put him in the patrol car and took him to jail. That was the vision I now had of my precious son. How could I have ever thought that would help us heal?

Marissa pled "not guilty" and was released back into the custody of Social Services; she spent only one night in jail. Colton was not so lucky since he had been arrested on a Friday; he spent the weekend in jail and was arraigned on Monday morning. He, too, was released back into the custody of Social Services after pleading "not guilty" as well, and now another wait began. We would be forced to wait several more months for the first court date.

The prosecuting attorney assured us he would ask for lie detector tests on both Marissa and Colton. They both fervently denied all of the allegations, so he wanted to be sure. We thought this would bring us some answers; but the results came back about a month later and were inconclusive. This seemed the most fitting result, no truth, no lies, just a world somewhere between the two, a world we had been living in for far too long.

The only good news was that they did not pass. We had not realized it, but this was important to Social Services; they were completing an internal investigation into what had happened. By summer they had concluded that both Colton and Marissa were guilty of the sexual abuse of their brother and ordered that both of them begin treatment. Our case-worker assured us that, regardless of what happened in court now, they were listed as sexual offenders within the department and would be treated accordingly. That was, of course, assuming they would remain in Social Service custody.

At this time the judge ruled in the neglect charges against Joe and me. He ruled that Colton and Marissa were "beyond our reasonable control, through no fault of our own." The county prosecutor spoke on our behalf at the hearing saying we had done all we could in trying to work out arrangements with the Dempster family to provide a home for Marissa and Colton. The neglect case was dropped, and we had survived one more inconceivably painful ordeal.

But about a week later I answered the door to a process server. He handed me a package, and I could not have been more confused. In it was a subpoena for us to appear before the state court; we were being charged with failure to pay child support. The state was suing us for support of both Colton and Marissa at their current placements. It was incredible to us that Colton, Marissa, and even the county department could have done so much to us. And once we were deemed inno-cent, there were no apologies, no "we were wrong," nothing except on to the next thing—attempting to force us to pay for the support until the age of twenty-one of two people who had raped our young son.

By July our family needed to get away. We decided to go on a vacation and pretend none of this happened. The best part was that we were going to be out of the country and we knew our phones would not work. We would be able to go almost two entire weeks without one call from the D.A., the caseworker, the therapist, the schools or anyone.

As soon as we arrived back in Miami after the trip and I checked my phone, I had a message from the prosecuting attorney's office. I was afraid to retrieve it—I was afraid of everything unknown at this point. The message stated that Marissa had run away from the group foster home in which she had been placed. My first thought was one of disappointment because I knew Marissa would not go back. I knew she would do all she could to avoid the upcoming court dates as well as the mandatory sexual offender's program. This disappointment faded as the next message on the phone was from the caseworker. She had called to inform us Marissa had been picked up a few days later on an outstanding warrant issued when she ran away. She was in the county jail and would be held there until her court date. We returned to Denver, knowing she would be held accountable for what she had done. Months went by as one court date and then another was postponed. Marissa's court-appointed lawyer seemed always to need more time. Meanwhile, Marissa sat in jail. As angry as I was at her I had no comfort in that. I knew I could not be there for her, but I was saddened she was alone.

For a while she kept in contact with Roseanne, who I suppose now believed in Marissa's innocence. At some point, though, she turned on Marissa. I do not know all the details but was told by the D.A. that Roseanne would no longer be involved with anything regarding this case. Roseanne later sought a restraining order on both Colton and Marissa. There was already a restraining order between Colton and Marissa and between Marissa and our family so she really was alone, or so we thought.

In the fall I received a phone call from Marissa's biological aunt Pam. I had met her eleven years earlier when we were going through the adoption process. Now that Marissa was eighteen Pam wanted to see her again. The county had told me she had originally applied to be the foster parent of Marissa, Colton and Willy all those years ago. She and her family did not pass the Social Service investigation, however, and were not considered an appropriate placement. Now she had hired a private investigator to find us and had driven by our home on many occasions. It was not a comforting thought in the midst of everything else that the biological family was following us. I did not tell her at first that Marissa no longer lived here. To do so would mean I would have to tell her Marissa was in jail. Instead I took down her information and sent it to Marissa's defense attorney. I was saddened that Pam would be the one to comfort Marissa through all of this instead of me. I had been her mom for ten years. I had held her, loved her, taught her to drive and talked to her about boys. I had been her mother, and now a restraining order against her prevented any contact between us. I did not want Pam to be with her, but I did not want Marissa to be alone even more. So I sent the information and in doing so complicated the entire situation dramatically by allowing the biological family back in.

Marissa did contact Pam, and they began a relationship; but Pam decided not to bail her out of jail. Marissa remained in custody through the fall and through the Christmas holiday. We again left the country at Christmas, and when we returned we were told someone had bailed Marissa out. We had no idea who, and the courts would not share that information with us. She was free, and we had no idea where she was.

On the other hand, Colton had been moved up north to a home for sexual perpetrators and was doing well, following the rules of treatment, attending school and making progress. We decided at that point no longer to attend the court hearings. They were too painful, and, except for our being witnesses in the actual trial, there was no point in our being there. It had now been months since we had seen either of our children. A tremendous feeling of loss always overshadowed the pain and anger.

It was now spring, a full year and a half after Johnny first told us the truth, and it was finally our day in court. Joe and I and Joey had been called as witnesses because Johnny had shared some information with Joey as to what Marissa had done to him only days after he had shared it with us. We sat in the hallway; as witnesses we were not allowed in the courtroom until our testimony. The D.A. came out and told us the defense attorney had asked for another continuance and the judge had allowed it; we went home. This happened twice more, with Joe taking off from work and Joey getting out of school. Each time the three of us prepared for the incredibly difficult task of testifying truthfully against someone we still loved.

I prayed on a continual basis that the Lord would see fit somehow to resolve this without our family's testimony. I could think of nothing worse than to sit on that witness stand, look down at my beautiful children and recount those horrible accusations against them—nothing worse, that is, than for Johnny to have to look at both of them as he testified about the years of abuse. Repeatedly I asked God for some kind of intervention; none came.

We were sitting in the hallway of the courthouse again, as was our routine, while Marissa's biological family walked back and forth into the courtroom avoiding eye contact with us. Suddenly the courtroom door opened, and a tall, very heavy, older black man came through it. At first Joe and I were so confused. This man, Max, had been a football coach of our boys years earlier. Over the past five years we'd had no real contact with him. He had always seemed like a nice person; he was married, had a child, and seemed to care about all the children. There he was standing in the courthouse, outside of Marissa's hearing. At first we were too stunned to speak. He walked down the hall to get a drink of water. When he came back he said, "Hey, how are you guys?"

Joe replied, "What are you doing here?" He said it in a voice that was evident he no longer knew what was real and what was not anymore.

Max answered in a nonchalant, confident way. "I'm here to support Marissa. I'm here for her."

This was just one more betrayal, one more deceit and one more question to which we would never know the answer. Just then the D.A. came out and told us Marissa had been granted yet another continuance and we would be subpoenaed again for the next court date. He went on to assure us we were free to go home. That was almost laughable. We knew of no home. It was only a house now, and we had not known freedom in almost two years.

We later learned that Max, once a friend of our family and someone we trusted, had bailed Marissa out. He and Marissa had been living together for the past months. He had left his wife and child because he was in love with our child. It was disturbing to us because Max knew Marissa when she was only eleven or twelve; now he was living with her. Why would he have an intimate relationship with someone he knew only as a little girl? Then again why would she have an intimate relationship with a little boy? I wondered if he believed she loved him. He must know she was only using him because she had no one else. He could not be that naïve; then I remembered we were.

Our search for justice was yielding no results. Court dates for both Colton and Marissa came and went. We waited, helpless and confused. When we thought our journey could get no darker, God showed us a light.

Caller ID read the courthouse. I answered it anyway. I had been avoiding those calls, but for some reason I picked it up. It was the new prosecuting attorney. He had replaced the former prosecutor about two months earlier. "Deb," he said. The first thing I noticed was that he did not have the "I have some bad news for you" tone in his voice.

"Yes," I hesitantly answered.

"Deb, Colton's attorney asked for a special hearing this afternoon."

"Another one?" I sighed.

"You don't understand. Colton pled guilty. He admitted what he did to Johnny, what he did to you, to your whole family. All I need is your approval on sentencing, and it will all be over."

As much as I knew it would never really be over, I was so thankful for this little hope. I sat down on the couch to catch my breath, not ready yet to believe this was true.

The attorney continued. "Colton has agreed to everything we asked. He will be sentenced as a juvenile. He will be placed on the sexual offender's list for ten years and attend a court-ordered, two-year sexual offenders' program. In addition, he will take mandatory lie-detector tests and either a false or inconclusive result will terminate his probation, and he will be sent to jail. He will remain in the custody of Social Services and continue treatment at the group home at which he has been placed. He will serve a minimum of two years of probation contingent on his success in treatment. Deb, do you agree to this?"

He wanted my answer, and all I wanted was to thank my son. He had caused us so much pain, and yet here he was offering the one thing I had begged God for so many times. He was making it possible for us not to have to go into court and testify against him. I wanted so much to hold him and thank him.

"Deb, there is one more thing. He has agreed to testify against Marissa at her trial. This will ensure a conviction; it may even encourage her to take a plea."

In my life, no one had ever given me a greater gift. We had not even begun the process of healing. This search for justice had consumed us, and yet it was over. Johnny would no longer need to fear testifying against Colton, and Joe, I, and Joey would never go back to that courthouse again on behalf of Colton. I was sad, but I do not know if I was sad because he had finally admitted what he had done, making it true, or sad because this court case was the only thing that still connected us to Colton. Now that it was over, we truly had to let him go. I told the attorney to accept the deal. I hung up and quietly said both thank you and good-bye to my son.

In a rather anticlimactic moment Marissa too pled guilty. Once she heard from her lawyer of Colton's plea and of his intention to testify against her, she had no other options. Unlike Colton, Marissa showed no remorse or even honesty; she pled because she thought she would be convicted. Colton had made some real progress in his healing. Marissa had made a good deal. Yet her sentence was the same as his.

Sometimes I feel there was justice for Colton. He stood in front of that courtroom and was able to admit remorsefully what he had done. He made the tough decision to end the pain of our family and accept the consequences for that. With Marissa there was no justice; she was aided and comforted by all those around her. She was enabled to continue with her deceit. She never felt any of our pain; she had only tried to spare her own.

Nevertheless, even if we had found justice for both of them, we would still have to accept that justice is not healing. I wonder how many people have passionately fought for the perpetrator in their life to receive a harsh sentence, even the death penalty, because they thought it would comfort their loss. In the end I am sure, like us, their pain was not lessened. Justice does not hold that power. The power of justice is righteousness, and the power of righteousness is the truth. The truth is all we can seek to begin healing.

Chapter Fourteen
Emotional Healing

~~~~~~~~~~~~~~~~~~~~~~~~~~~~~~~~~~~~

Ecclesiastes 3:3
"A time to kill and a time to heal,
a time to tear down and a time to build."

~~~~~~~~~~~~~~~~~~~~~~~~~~~~~~~~~~~~

I sat back down in the rocking chair to rest for a moment. The memories of our life were so difficult, and I had repressed so much. I wondered if anyone in our family would ever have true healing or if we would just make it day to day until the pain numbed us into a false sense of wellness.

As I rocked in the chair I looked around at both the progress I had made and how much I had left to do. Outwardly the veranda was changing; it was taking on a less neglected and damaged appearance. To a passerby its beauty was returning. Still, for those who knew it before, who knew the immense beauty it could hold, it was pale in comparison. The renovation would have to go deeper, and as it did, it would likely reveal more areas that needed to be addressed.

I continued to rock as I contemplated our many attempts at healing and why sometimes we made progress and sometimes we seemed to sink deeper into our sadness, with our wounds only becoming more visible. In the end I think it was simple; we were caught between wanting to heal, by letting go of the pain, and wanting to hold on to it because we did not want to let go of Colton and Marissa. If we no longer grieved them, they would truly be gone.

I have often heard it said that grief has many stages. Elizabeth Kubler-Ross identified them as denial, anger, bargaining, depression and acceptance. It sounded so easy, step by step; but I, like many people, misinterpreted the healing process. Feelings went back and forth for each of us; from day to day we were at different places. Angry one moment, depressed at another and then denying any of it was possible the next. My biggest misinterpretation would be that when we accomplished all five of those stages we would be healed.

The truth is that acceptance, the last stage of grief, is only the first stage in true grief work. Grief work has been associated with the acronym TEAR—*to* accept the reality of the loss, *e*xperience the pain of the loss, *a*djust to the new environment without the lost object and *r*einvest in the new reality. We were so far from that. We were just accepting what had happened to us. We could not imagine a reality that did not include them. It is incredibly difficult to heal when you cannot envision what the result of that healing would look like.

It is equally difficult to heal when there are so many reasons not to. I still wanted to be angry with the people who abandoned us. I wanted to hold on to the resentment I had toward Social Services. I wanted to stay in this dark place because I still held on to the fantasy that both Colton and Marissa would come back, and if I were healed they would not know how much I truly loved them. I had reasons for wanting to hold on to the grief and lack of forgiveness, but in my Christian spirit I knew the reasons to let go of them were so much greater. As the mother of this family I also knew it was my responsibility to make sure each of us found forgiveness for, and acceptance of, what had happened to us and each of us let go of this pain.

It was immediately obvious we would all need to heal in our own way, but Johnny had to be the priority. He needed help in processing everything that had happened. He still believed Marissa was in love with him and the sex was only an act of her love toward him. He also believed she would come back for him because they were going to be together again someday. He missed her, and he struggled with guilt about telling the truth. Some days he believed he made the right decision, and other days he very much regretted it. More than anything he had been so apprehensive and frightened about the upcoming trial. We had no idea where to start with the intense therapy he would need.

We first took Johnny to a therapist our insurance company recommended. This therapy was designed for far less complicated matters, and no one was more uncomfortable than the therapist about the subject matter.

The three of us told our story, each from our own place of pain. Johnny from the point of his love for Marissa, Joe from his place of confusion and betrayal, and me from my place of guilt.

"We took Johnny into our home to protect him from the abuse he was suffering in his biological family and to offer him opportunity; yet the abuse happened in our home. He was less safe with us than he was with them. We should have known what was going on," I began.

Suddenly Johnny was comforting me; he stood up, walked over to my chair and wrapped his arms around me. I should have been the one to console him, and yet he was reassuring me. Joe, Johnny and I continued taking turns telling our individual truths, fully aware none of us knew the actual truth. When we finally finished telling the therapist our story, her only response was, "I am in way over my head."

She told us she did not believe she had the expertise to deal with such an intense and complicated manner. What she was sure of was that each of us needed individual counseling. She sent us away with only the promise she would call us back in a few days with the name of someone who might be able to help us. We had told one more person our secret and once again to no avail.

It did not take a few days as she had assured us; it took a few weeks. But when she finally called she referred us to a therapist who dealt only with sexual abuse. We made the appointment and the very long drive, and finally, hesitantly, we entered through a wrought iron gate a building in downtown Denver. It was an old row house converted to a small office. With Johnny by our side we walked into the waiting room. To our surprise it was filled with grown men, each starring at us as if we had walked into the wrong building.

In time a man who seemed to be in a position of authority entered the room and informed those waiting that group was about to begin. With that, they arose and followed him into a conference room. We waited for about fifteen more minutes listening to the quiet sounds of piped-in music that was meant to sedate. Finally the therapist entered. I spoke with her alone for a moment about my concern over the men in the waiting room and the fact that I had overheard them talking about this meeting as a requirement of their probation.

She informed me they held meetings for sexual perpetrators at this office as well as intense psychosexual therapy for many of the men who had been convicted. It seemed unfathomable to me that we were asked to bring our young child into a therapist's office, that by her own admission was full of pedophiles; yet we continued to attend. I look back, and I cannot imagine what we were thinking to make this all right in our minds; we were following blindly, for lack of any instinct of our own. We attended for several more months, and although I saw absolutely no progress on Johnny's part I noticed Willy was greatly affected. Johnny had asked Willy to join him in therapy because he felt they shared some of the same memories. Willy was reluctant but finally agreed.

From the moment the office door was shut at the first meeting Willy began to cry. He did this for the next hour and for every meeting after that. He said many honest and profound things, but it would remain the first thing he said on the first day that hit me the hardest.

"I have lost my confidence," he said, sobbing.

He elaborated further by saying he did not believe in himself anymore. He said he struggled at school, in sports and even in his relationship with us. That made me sad because I felt some responsibility for that. I tried so hard to ensure that Willy would not feel the repercussion of the acts of his brother and sister. The pain they had caused was not his to bear. But the truth was, I was trying to make myself believe that as much as I was trying to make him, and he sensed that. At times he sounded like them, he had their mannerisms, and he looked like them. He was a very real reminder of our pain, but he was not the source of it. He was just one more of their victims. I knew that in my heart and on a conscious level in my mind; but at times, many at first, I had to remind myself of that.

Willy was able to let go of much pain in these sessions. He revealed many secrets he had hidden for so many years. He spoke of the manipulation and control Marissa and Colton held over him and was honest about his part in the deceit. The healing came from letting go of the secrets. Johnny was silent as he watched with the sadness that comes from wanting something you know you will never have. Willy wanted healing, and he wanted support in that effort. His wound, although equally painful, was somehow not as deep as Johnny's and was therefore more accessible. Willy strove to reach that pain; Johnny had already made the decision, conscious or not, that he, himself, could never get there.

In healing it became important to acknowledge the primary source of pain for each of us, and it was different for each one. For Amy, the pain was in the betrayal she felt by Navin, the youth pastor of our church, as well as by the other young people in the youth group. It was strange. Colton and Marissa came forward with their allegations, and everyone in Amy's life took a step back.

For Amy, healing would be found in writing a letter to Navin. She knew, even as she wrote it, that he would never respond. But it was important he know how hurt she was by his ostracizing her. She trusted him. I was afraid she would have trouble trusting anyone in a church situation like this again if he did not respond. Unfortunately, as she antici- pated, he did not respond. She wrote him one more time; she just needed to write the words to let them go. I am not sure if she mailed that letter or not; it doesn't matter. It was in the writing that she found healing.

Amanda moved into her own apartment. It was probably best at the time because the stress of what was happening at home was so difficult for her, and dealing with it at the same time as going to college was next to impossible. In the end, though, this delayed her healing. She would not begin to deal with it until nearly two years later when in an almost unbe- lievable coincidence she moved into her dream apartment and found out Marissa was living in the apartment directly under her. Marissa had moved in with Max and was pregnant with his baby. Amanda asked the leasing agent how they could let a registered pedophile move in. They responded by saying the apartment was in Max's name and he had informed them Marissa was his daughter and was pregnant with his grand- daughter. Amanda shared the truth with the agent. This was the first time she had ever spoken those words to anyone and in doing so found some healing. Marissa and Max's lease was not renewed, and Amanda stayed in the apartment she had looked so forward to. In the end there was no running away from this pain, not for any of us.

Joey and Paul dealt with it in a much less visible way. They hid their feelings in an effort to regain some kind of normalcy. I think they wanted Joe and me not to worry about them through all this, so they in many ways supported us. I believe they were much better at not personalizing what happened and at seeing it as the mistakes of Colton and Marissa rather than their own. They were able to distance themselves from the shame and guilt that some of us bore and were able outwardly to speak of their anger. In the end they worked through it with no therapeutic intervention.

I would find out later, though, that both of them on their school spiritual retreats had individually found the courage to share their story with their peers, their teachers, their advisers and their priests. In their moments of testimony, almost two years apart, they each told of their pain, betrayal and loss. They were supported and cared for by other young men who had only seen them as popular, confident and well liked. Both Joey and Paul had been seen as fierce competitors in sports and gentle souls at school, but no one knew the depth of the pain they carried. Once they did, they never let either Paul or Joey shoulder it alone again.

Joe dealt with it as he did with any crisis in our marriage and our family. He was our protector, the one who would make everything right again if we just trusted him, and we did. He comforted us at the same time as he sought justice for what happened. I remember when we were first married and I sometimes wished Joe was more the sensitive type. Instead he was the perfect strong man. Finally I understood; it was his strength that would save our family. Joe never shed a tear; he only wiped ours. He took complete control of the situation, and we followed his lead. He came to every therapy appointment with every child. He went to every court date, sometimes alone because I did not have the strength to go.

He sought answers to every question and was solely responsible for our family being able to survive.

I only saw him break down once. Joey and Paul left for the football game a couple of hours early so they could get dressed and warm up on the field. Later, when we arrived, we were told they were not there yet. We panicked and wondered if they had been involved in an accident on the way over. Joe looked at me with the saddest, most hopeless expression I had ever seen and said, "If something happened to my boys, I will never forgive God. He and I are through." Fortunately the boys were fine and merely lost in an area they were unfamiliar with. But I understood then that, although Joe had forgiven God, he was not emotionally or spiritually able to accept any more pain. He still needed healing of his own.

I continued with therapy, even up to two years after this happened. It was difficult for me because I held on to my grief; it was the "tie that binds." I also continued to struggle with my loss of reputation even though my therapist often reminded me that- reputation is rarely proportioned to virtue; still I missed it. However, in time I accepted that loss and in doing so discovered what an impediment it had been and how freeing it was without it.

As for the grief, something began to change for me after my therapist gave me an article on psychopathic personality. It was his opinion that not only were both Marissa and Colton psychopaths, but in his estimation, they were the two most dangerous children we had raised. He wanted me to accept this for a couple of reasons. One, he felt if I understood the mind of a psychopath I would understand that what had happened had little to do with us and everything to do with them. Two, I would understand how truly lucky my family was to have survived living with them for over ten years.

The article from www.oregoncounseling.org, March 2004, stated, "A psychopath never remains attached to anyone or anything. They live a 'predatory' lifestyle. They feel little or no regret and little or no remorse—except when they are caught. They need relationships but see people as obstacles to overcome and be eliminated. If not, they see people in terms of how they can be used. They use people for stimulation, to build their self-esteem, and they invariably value people in terms of their material value." The article goes on to state, "They can be expert in manipulating others by playing to their emotions. There is a shallow quality to the emotional aspect of their stories."

Further, the article provided a list of items based on the research of Robert Hare, Ph.D., derived from "The Hare Psychopathy Checklist—Revised 1991, Toronto: Multi-Health Systems, The checklist included:

glibness/ superficial charm	grandiose sense of self worth
need for stimulation/ prone to boredom	pathological lying
conning/ manipulative	lack of remorse or guilt
shallow emotional response	callous/ lack of empathy
parasitic lifestyle	poor behavior controls
promiscuous sexual behavior	early behavior problems

lack of realistic long-terms goals	impulsivity
irresponsibility	failure to accept responsibility for their own actions
many short-term relationships	juvenile delinquency
revocation of conditional release	criminal versatility

I read the entire article and began to understand that psychopathy involves poor emotional intelligence, the lack of conscience and an inability to attach. The most surprising aspect of the article stated that "there may be a genetic influence that creates a psychopathic personality."

In reading the article and discussing it in depth with my therapist, as well as doing additional research on my own, I saw he was right. Both Marissa and Colton had psychopathic personalities. In truly understanding and accepting this, it became easier to forgive myself for my inability to make this situation right.

In addition, Joe and I began attending a group sponsored by Social Services for parents recovering from sexual abuse of their child by a family member. The class was difficult but it did help us to come to terms with what had happened in our home. I could not help but to wonder though how much more effective this class would have been if it was preventative instead of reactive. Even so, the support was encouraging. When sexual abuse occurred in our home, we felt like we were the only one to whom it had ever happened; we felt isolated and alone. In these sessions, we were able to share our pain and feel the pain of others, who too, had discovered the awful "secret" that existed in their families. We dreaded these meetings; conversely, we were always glad we went.

We all silently struggled, but we were able to find one thing that seemed to work for everybody—travel. We began spending more and more time away from home, especially at the holidays. We climbed Dunne's River Falls in Jamaica, went cave tubing in Belize and hiked the rain forests of Central America. We went line-zipping across the jungles of Costa Rica, spent time with the Embera Indian tribe on an island off Panama, and spent weeks at a time in Mexico. Unfortunately we were in New Orleans when hurricane Katrina hit, but we were not afraid. We were together, and regardless of what we were experiencing we found healing in our togetherness. We began to look for adventure everywhere and had no trouble finding it. We let go of all our individual fears; if we had survived what had happened to us, we had nothing left to fear.

We even opened ourselves up to going on mission trips again. This was difficult because we had found healing and solace within our family. We had become extremely close, and the thought of allowing anyone else in was disturbing. Still we knew God had called us for more, and if we did not at least take some steps toward that now, we never would. Our first mission trip was only a week to a Lakota Indian Reservation in South Dakota, and we went as a family. We thought this would be good for us because it was not a long-term commitment; we could work for a week and then move on. In the end, it was unrealistic for us to think that was possible, because that was not who we were or are. We made friendships and commitments to families we met there that we still keep. When we finally found the courage to open our hearts again we could not possibly put any limitation on it. This was only the beginning of our missionary work.

By outward appearance it would seem our family was beginning to find some healing; then again we had been deceived by appearances before.

Chapter Fifteen
Split with Reality

~~~~~~

Galatians 4:14
"Even though my illness was a trial to you,
you did not treat me with contempt or scorn.
Instead, you welcomed me as if I
were an angel of God,
as if I were Christ Jesus himself."

~~~~~~

I was beginning to remember the beauty this porch once held; I loved the idea of bringing that back into existence. It was missing only one thing, water. I needed to fill the fountains and birdbaths and water all the new growth. I also needed to spray down the last remains of the dust that had once hidden its beauty. Water is life. I knew that with water this sanctuary would again breathe life. I thought about the incredible healing power of water and that what this family needed more than anything now was to continue with the healing. Unfortunately there is also another aspect to water; it has the power to reveal that which is hidden. I was frightened that in our journey to find healing more truths would be revealed, truths that would be difficult to accept.

The last week of March, while I was at home working in the study, I received a phone call. It was from the principal of Johnny's elementary school, and she had Johnny in her office. She was very concerned because he had approached his teacher, Ms. Black, with a letter he had found in his desk. The letter threatened him, his friends and his family; Johnny was frightened and went to Ms. Black crying. It caught her attention because she knew that both Marissa and Desiree had tried, on more than one occasion, to get into Willy's middle school in an effort to sway his testimony on what was to be the upcoming trial. She knew we were forced, with the district providing the necessary documentation, to seek a restraining order against Desiree because she had gotten into Willy's classroom after being turned away at the front entrance.

Johnny had been fearful of the same thing happening to him, and we had advised the school of this possibility. Our concern was deepened by the fact that Johnny's class was located in a mobile unit behind the school. The mobile was locked at all times; still it did not seem to offer the same degree of safety as the school.

The principal said, "I think you need to come down to the school immediately, with your husband if possible."

I hung up and called Joe. He was home within a few minutes, and we left for the school. When we entered the principal's office we were brought into a conference room. At the table sat Johnny, his teacher, the school psychologist, the assistant principal and the special-ed teacher. Each was trying in his or her own way to find the underlying truth behind this letter.

The first thing we were asked was if we wanted to contact the police department. We said yes, but first we would like to know a little more about what happened and how whoever had done this was able to access the classroom when we had been assured it was locked at all times.

The principal again guaranteed us the door had remained locked, which added to the mystery of how the letter could have been placed in Johnny's desk. Further, it was obvious from the questions Johnny, Joe and I were being asked that the school was somewhat hesitant to believe this story. Johnny had a look of sadness, but there was something else; I was unsure what.

I was confused because there also seemed to be something more on the school's part that they were not sharing with us.

"May I please see the letter?" I finally asked.

I was horrified at what I saw. The letter contained both profanity and inconceivable threats. The threats were against Johnny, Johnny's teacher and his fellow classmates. My eyes were drawn to the fact that the handwriting seemed to change so much from the beginning of the letter to the end. The printing became larger and the pencil marks darker as the letter progressed. It looked to me as if anger and rage were building as the words were being written. It almost had a kind of psychotic look to it. It contained threats of violence and even cannibalism. It frightened me that anyone could write such a letter, especially to a child.

Before Joe and I even had the time to process what we had just read, the school psychologist interrupted us.

"Mr. and Mrs. Hannah, there is no way someone could have gotten in to Johnny's desk. We searched his desk and found what we considered some violent drawings and further took a handwriting sample. Unfortunately the handwriting on the letter has some real similarities to Johnny's other work."

"What are you saying?" Joe asked.

"Is it possible Johnny wrote the letter to himself?" she responded.

"Why would he do that?" I questioned.

"Perhaps it is the only way he could get his feelings out. Maybe he just wanted everyone else to know how horrible he feels, and this is the only way he knew to reach out," the principal responded.

"I need to talk to him alone. I'll know if he is telling the truth," I said sadly.

With that, Joe and I took Johnny into the other room and asked him to tell us everything that happened. There were obvious holes in the story, but his mannerisms told even more. It took about twenty minutes, but Johnny was finally able to find the courage to admit he had written the letter.

With that information we went back into the other room, and Johnny admitted what had really happened although he would not say why.

The school psychologist said, "Obviously Johnny needs some serious help. He will of course need to be suspended from school because of the threats made against other students and teachers. We will do some testing on him after the suspension and decide where to go from there. For now you need to take him home, and you are welcome to take home these other drawings we found in his desk as well."

Joe, Johnny and I stood up, but the truth was none of us had any idea where we would go from there. I looked at the door and was frightened by the aspect of walking through it and leaving what I considered the sound advice of professionals and instead relying on our own, already damaged instincts.

I turned around. "What should we do?" I asked.

"Get him the help he needs. We'll be in touch."

None of us spoke in the car, and Johnny walked directly up to his room when we arrived home. Joe and I began to discuss the depth of Johnny's needs. We decided we would speak to him together and try to find out where we should go from there.

We called Johnny down and first assured him we were not angry. He was surprised since he had just been suspended from school. We asked him to be honest with us about what was really going on. He said calmly, "I feel like I wish I had not been born, I wish I didn't exist, and I wish other people did not exist."

Joe and I questioned him about the violence toward his friends that he wrote of in the letter. His answer was simple. "They were never my friends." He said they would wait for him inside the mobile and beat him up before the teacher came in, and he was afraid of going to school because he knew they would hurt him.

We knew this was not possible; the mobile was locked until the teacher came to unlock it and let all the students in at one time. "Johnny, that is not true. You know that is not true, don't you?" I pleaded.

He put his head down and shook it.

Joe and I became increasingly confused as the conversation continued. Johnny made statement after statement we knew not to be true. He did not appear to be lying; instead he appeared as confused as we were. Sitting on my couch was this little boy whose fear was so intense I felt it.

"I promise you we will do everything we can to help you. You need to trust that," I said.

It was obvious he did not believe it, not even for a moment. Still I had to do something. I called the local mental health facility for some type of guidance. I was told to take him in for an emergency psych evaluation to determine his level of safety. I followed up on that advice but was informed we could not get him in until the following morning. I feared it was going to be a very long night. I was wrong; Johnny was tired and wanted to lie down. He cried himself to sleep; I checked on him several times, but he seemed to sleep through the night.

Amy and Joey asked if they could take the day off from school to go to the psychiatrist with Johnny because they were worried about him; we allowed it. The five of us left, not knowing what was coming next. The psychiatrist talked with Johnny alone for what seemed like an eternity; then she called Joe and me back.

"Johnny is experiencing psychosis. We consider it of unknown origin at this time. He will need to be hospitalized for further testing," the doctor stated with authority.

"Psychosis? I don't understand. How do you know it is psychosis?" Joe asked.

"Johnny was acting on the commands of voices he said he was hearing when he wrote the note. He wasn't actually commanded to write the letter, though. Instead he was commanded to commit those heinous acts. He tried to appease the voices by writing the letter and directing the anger toward himself instead of toward others," she said.

I looked over at Johnny. "Do you hear voices?"

He nodded his head and began to sob.

"It appears Johnny has heard the voices for quite some time. They seem to be growing stronger and more violent now, and he can no longer control them. It was right to bring him here; we'll get him the help he needs," she concluded.

The next few hours were filled with meeting with other psychiatrists, completing the commitment papers and arranging for a bed. We were blessed to find an opening in a reputable mental hospital designated only for children and were informed we could take him right over.

We tried to assure Johnny this was the best thing for him, but by this time he had completely disconnected. He stared blankly out the window as if he was fully aware that the life he once knew would never be the same. We stopped to get something for lunch although none of us were hungry.

It was heartbreaking after all Johnny had endured; it was evident he felt that we, too, were abandoning him. In actuality, our confidence in our own decision-making abilities had been so shaken that we were still following blindly the advice of others. Once we arrived we had several more hours of interviews, paperwork and examinations. By the time we left late that evening we were exhausted. Johnny did not cry when we left; he, like us, had no tears left.

The following morning I had a conversation with the psychiatrist on call for the weekend. He had finished his initial session with Johnny. He said that based on Johnny's biological history as well as his symptoms he was giving the diagnosis of psychosis of unknown origin; but it was his opinion Johnny was suffering from childhood-onset schizophrenia. He felt it was too early to label him with that diagnosis, but we should be aware that it was a definite possibility.

It was exactly what we had all feared. The psychiatrist informed us that extreme trauma could cause this kind of early onset. He also said Johnny in all likelihood would have still suffered from schizophrenia; but the sexual abuse and admission of the truth probably made it appear much sooner than it would have otherwise.

For the next ten days test after test was performed on Johnny. He began taking antipsychotic medication as well as an antidepressant and mood stabilizer. We went to visit him every day even though it was over an hour drive each way. Johnny talked honestly and openly to us about not only the strange voices but also hallucinations. He spoke of extremely paranoid thoughts and a definite desire to hurt not only himself but also others. Then we were told to take him home.

"You will need to adjust your lives accordingly. Put an alarm on his door to track his whereabouts. Meet with the school; with these kinds of violent thoughts they probably will not let him back in. Continue with medication and therapy and develop a safety plan for your family." The discharge counselor said those words as if they had no implication.

"I don't understand," Joe said. "Johnny himself states that neither he nor anyone in the family is safe if the voices command him to do something. How can you send him back home?"

"This is a hospital. We deal only with crisis situations, and long-term care will be your responsibility. Don't forget to stop and fill his prescription for the antipsychotic medica-

tion on the way home and meet with his outpatient psychiatrist within the next two days," she concluded.

We turned to each other and waited for the click of the
door being unlocked from inside the booth. "Good luck,"
she called out.

Luck! We had a child who had been sexually abused for
the last five years, was hearing voices and seeing things that
were not there, and wanted to hurt himself and everyone
around him. No, luck was not going to do it this time.

They were right about one thing; the school did not think
it was in the best interest of everyone involved for Johnny
to return. A teacher was sent to our house for the remaining
two months of the school year. She worked with Johnny on
an individual basis, but this was a temporary situation until
we could work out something else.

That something else included the long process of getting
Johnny accepted into a day-treatment program through the
mental health agency. During that time his medication was
changed a couple of times and several more drugs were
added. He struggled through the summer, and we all looked
forward to the fall. During the previous six months we had
not had even one moment when we were not with him.

Fall did come, and Johnny, although not appearing to
make progress, was able to maintain in this new day-treatment setting. The classes were extremely small, only four to
six kids. A psychiatrist, a psychologist, a teacher and an aide
were available at any given time. The structure was good
for Johnny, and for a while we thought he might eventually
become successful in this environment.

At home Johnny was not maintaining. His behavior
became more and more bizarre. He was extremely angry
about the alarm on his door. He became obsessed with
that thought as well as how he could bypass the alarm. He
directed his anger at the people he felt were trying to control
him, our family and his therapists and doctors. He also began

to cut himself. We had been careful to remove from his room anything we thought he could use as a weapon. In a small hole, where a picture had been removed, Johnny hid a nail he would later use against himself.

He did not need a weapon, though; once he used an eraser to erase a hole in his arm. It was about the size of a quarter and deep enough to go through all the layers of his skin and cause substantial bleeding. He said he had a power no one else had; he did not feel pain, and no matter what he did to himself or what others did to him he could not feel it.

One time I went into Johnny's room, and he was lying on the bed, staring at the ceiling. I sat down on the floor next to him and laid my head on his bed. I just wanted him to know he was not alone. We talked a little about nothing important. But then I happened to glance over at the edge of the bed. The bed skirt was pulled up, and I saw in a perfect line about ten small paper cups filled with some type of liquid. I asked Johnny, "What are those?" He did not respond. I reached under and pulled one out, and to my horror it was filled with urine.

"Johnny, why are these here?" I asked.

He began to cry. "I don't know why I put them there. I just had to," he said with confusion.

I cleaned those up, but that was not the last time they appeared under the bed. The sad part was that Johnny was as puzzled as we were as to why he did some of the things he did. He had other symptoms as well; he suffered from poor hygiene. His braces, which we had put on the previous year, had to be removed because of his refusal to brush his teeth; they were rotting underneath. We pleaded with him since we knew that if they were removed, his teeth would never be corrected, but that meant nothing to him. In addition his hair had to be buzzed because of his refusal to wash it.

We tried everything. But since Johnny had been so violated in the past it was unfathomable that we enter the bathroom while he was in there. He refused to change his clothes and often wore the same ones for a week. He also layered them on top of each other. He might have a thin gym pant, followed by a pair of jeans and then followed by a sweat pant. I questioned him; he would say only that he feared getting cold, even if it was in the middle of summer. Joe and I later learned this is not uncommon with children who have been sexually abused. Sometimes we did not know if a certain behavior was attributed to the sexual abuse or to the mental illness.

Johnny not only loved his time alone but also in some ways needed it. I wondered if he purposely got himself into trouble so he would be sent to his room. He began to seek isolation, and his anxiety level grew when he did not have access to it.

Johnny continued with individual and group therapy at the day treatment program, and Joe and I participated with him in family therapy. As we were nearing the end of another school year it became evident that, despite the efforts of some very skilled professionals, Johnny had made no real progress.

At a meeting with the psychiatrist we were informed that Johnny would need some additional testing. Dr. Ashley asked us to obtain this by taking Johnny to the Schizophrenic Research Institute at the University of Colorado Health Science Center. Dr. Ashley now, too, believed we were dealing with childhood onset schizophrenia. Joe and I agreed to the testing. When I look back, though, it seems both of us were in denial about the truth.

Within two weeks we were scheduled at the hospital. This was in fact a research project, but the main benefit for us would be an actual diagnosis. A staff assistant interviewed the three of us, and then Joe and I met with Dr. Rosenberg, a leader in diagnosis and treatment of childhood onset schizophrenia. We went through the entire history of absolutely everything we knew. He asked us so many questions—some we could see the relevance to; others we could not. After an exhausting session we were asked to leave and have Johnny come in. Dr.

Rosenberg spoke with him for about an hour and then sent Johnny for additional testing while he spoke with us.

"I am absolutely confident in giving you the diagnosis of childhood onset schizophrenia. I do not believe there is any doubt," he said.

I had to catch my breath. It is one thing to suspect it, but quite another to receive the actual diagnosis.

"I see many children each week who have been referred to me because of some suspicion on their therapist's part. I diagnose fewer than ten percent of these children. Childhood schizophrenia is extremely rare, but with the trauma Johnny suffered it is certainly reasonable," he continued.

Neither Joe nor I spoke a word. I do not even remember our looking at each other; we just stared at the floor. Finally I said, "How do you know?"

"Well, the voices are certainly concerning. Johnny spoke to me very openly about what they were saying, how he responded to them and the increasingly threatening nature of their commands.

Another concerning point is his increasing social with-drawal. Nothing matters to him anymore. He also has signs of paranoia, delusions of grandeur and great feelings of doom. The lack of personal hygiene is quite frequent with our patients. The violent tendencies are not necessarily characteristic of schizophrenia, but his feelings of wanting to hurt himself are. Approximately twelve percent of schizophrenic patients end up committing suicide; it is a great concern.

Further, I believe Johnny has the capacity to be violent toward others and toward himself. This will need to be moni-tored on a continual basis. I would ask you to come back next week for some further testing. I would like to do some blood work, some brain wave testing and some other reactive tests. This is only for research purposes and not diagnostic."

"That's a lot to take in," Joe mumbled as he shook his head.

"It is, but you must have had some indication," Dr. Rosenberg said.

"We did, but maybe we didn't want to face it. We'll bring him for the additional testing," I said as we left.

We went back, and Johnny finished with the testing. The diagnosis also included oppositional defiance disorder, childhood onset conduct disorder and attention deficit disorder, inattentive type.

We took this report back to the day-treatment program. We finally had the diagnosis; we each had accepted it—well, except for Johnny. There was a contradiction between his anger at having the same illness from which his mother had suffered, and his ability now to use this as a rationalization or justification for his current behavior.

He read each article Dr. Rosenberg and his office had given us. He liked the idea that his behavior was no longer so bizarre—at least not in the world of schizophrenia. He understood his antisocial behavior and now accepted it. He embraced his lack of personal hygiene and the voices in his head. It was almost as if he had known all along and was only now freed by our knowing.

What Johnny had tried to hide to fit into our world no longer needed to be hidden. He openly discussed wanting us dead. He drew pictures of the family dead and his therapist dead. He admitted he had been bypassing his alarm and going in Amy's room in the middle of the night, and he also admitted his fantasy of cutting off all of her hair while she was sleeping. He talked about how people were watching him from another planet and how he had powers that none of us had. His greatest power, he reiterated, was that he felt no pain. No matter what happened to him, it did not hurt. He would demonstrate by trying to cut himself or pinch himself, and then he would just laugh.

He continued in day treatment, and Joe and I continued with his therapy there. But even they had noticed a difference.

Johnny was sinking further and further, and the worst part was he was no longer trying to stay afloat. He had accepted his drowning and was only waiting for us to do the same.

Within two weeks it became evident that Johnny had become a real threat to himself and to others. His "hit list" had grown, and his details of death became meticulous. A decision was made at day-treatment that Johnny would need to be hospitalized, and so on May 2nd, 2005 he was taken by ambulance from the school to Ft. Lewis Mental Hospital.

The diagnosis, early onset schizophrenia, most likely brought on at this age by the trauma of the sexual abuse he had suffered. He was also diagnosed with post-traumatic stress disorder. He was kept at the hospital for about two weeks and then transferred to a residential treatment program that could meet his severe needs.

Johnny made it clear he did not want to come home. Then again why would he? He had been abused and abandoned by everyone in his life before he came to us. Then just as he was beginning to trust us these terrible things started happening to him, and we did not protect him. We were just more people on his list of those who had betrayed him. Maybe the best we could do for him at this time was to give him his wish and not make him come home. It was curious, however. He claimed repeatedly he did not want to talk with us, but he would call to tell us that on a daily basis. He would say he did not want to call us yet would panic if he did and we were not home. He said he did not want to see us yet worked very hard to earn the privilege to have visits. He said he hated us but would smile when we told him we loved him. He said he did not want to be touched by anyone, especially us, but would reach out for a hug when we would leave.

I started to understand he was angry at this disease. He was angry at the thought that it had been brought on sooner by what Colton and Marissa had done to him. He was angry at Colton and Marissa, and he was angry with Joe, me and the other kids for not knowing what was happening to him and not protecting him from it. But he did not hate us. He was angry with us because we could not make this better.

Johnny would not come back home. Schizophrenia is a complex and disturbing disease and one that put a claim on his future. We each had to mourn for what was not to be. We sometimes had to fight our own tears during visits for this little boy who had such a tough break in life. His appearance changed dramatically those first few months; he gained seventy pounds in the first year he left, although not much height. Yet when I looked in his eyes he was the same little boy. Johnny continued to struggle through different medications. At times he was so frightened of the voices he had no control over, and at times he was so sedated.

Johnny has now been moved from the hospital to a Catholic Group Home run by the Sisters of Charity. This was a good move and one well thought out and planned by his caseworker. This is his third caseworker since coming forward with the truth and although each was concerned with his well-being, this caseworker took into account not only his individual needs but also the needs of the entire family. We are excited about the possibility of growth and healing in this new environment. Still we keep his whereabouts secret because recently Marissa has reached out to Cain and others in an effort to reconnect with Johnny.

We continue to take him for short outings, ice cream and bowling. He also likes going to the pet store and holding the little animals, especially the ferrets. He enjoys going out to eat or just spending time with us. We, too, enjoy spending time with him, and even Mandy and Joey make it a priority to go out to visit him, even though it is hours from their colleges. We each do all we can to assure Johnny we will be with him forever. We will never abandon him. And we do this, not out of a sense of guilt because of what had happened to him in our home, but simply out of our tremendous love for him.

Recently Johnny has once again begun to acknowledge his love for us. He was taught for so many years not to trust us, and now that wall is crumbling under the weight of truth. He has begun calling us just to tell us he loves us; he eagerly waits for our visits and phones sometimes several times a day. He finally realizes he has a family. Even though we made a terrible mistake in not knowing what was happening to him and in not protecting him, he has given us his forgiveness. What an incredible gift that turned out to be, for by his forgiveness we could begin the long process of trying to forgive ourselves.

Chapter Sixteen
Spiritual Healing

I could not help but feel empowered by what we had survived, and yet I knew that power was fleeting. I picked up the bag of birdseed and began to fill the feeder. It occurred to me that, although this would feed the hungry birds, it would soon empty and need to be refilled. The birds would come back repeatedly, needing to be fed. What if they had grown to depend on this and when I neglected them for so long they did not know where to go to be fed? That was what I was experiencing spiritually. I had been fed for so many years by my Father, and now I was in the midst of neglecting that relationship and did not know where to go to be fed.

We had found emotional healing, even through Johnny's crisis, but we were not healed. Something was missing from who we once were. Our journey was not yet complete for there was still a wound that needed healing.

I have heard so many people speak of being angry with God, and I in my arrogance was so proud of the fact that I felt I had not been. Nevertheless, the truth is that the opposite of love is not hate; hate is only a passionate response. The opposite of love is indifference. George Bernard Shaw once wrote, "The worst sin toward our fellow creatures is not to hate them, but to be indifferent to them: that's the essence of inhumanity." I had applied that inhumanity toward God. What I was doing was so much worse than being angry; I was apathetic. Maybe I was afraid to explore my relationship with God any deeper because I was afraid of what I would find—that God should have protected us.

I think that alone has to be one of the biggest misconceptions of Christianity. If we do God's work with a humble and willing heart and all for His glory, He will protect us. I am not sure why I started believing that; it is certainly not scriptural. Scripture teaches us we will be mocked and ridiculed for the sake of our faith. Why had I overlooked the martyrs, John the Baptist, the apostles, even Job?

First Peter 4:12-13 states, "Dear friends, do not be surprised at the painful trial you are suffering, as though something strange were happening to you. But rejoice that you participate in the sufferings of Christ, so that you may be overjoyed when his glory is revealed." The truth is that the closer we are to God and the more willing we are to do His work, the more danger we are in. I guess in my immaturity I always looked for grace. I did not look for discipline or authority, simply grace. I had now learned something I feared would change my relationship with God forever. I had to accept that my Father would not always protect me, and I knew I would rather live in this state of aloneness than face that.

I would always say there were so many people who would do far greater things for Christ, there were so many people who lived a more pure and obedient life, and there were so many people who would devote more to God than I. But no one, and I meant no one, could love Him more. I felt a personal, intimate relationship with God. I knew Him and He knew me, and yet now I felt His betrayal as well. He could have stopped it; He could have left our hearts intact. He could have had someone stand up with us when we had to face it. But He left us alone, accused and betrayed. There was no way to put that reality into my faith so I ignored Him; but in a perfect paradox, I missed Him.

Much like a disagreement with anyone, I knew I needed to do the hard work of reconciling, but it always seemed as if it would be fine to wait just a little longer. The truth is that I was mad at God and in my passive aggressiveness thought I was hurting Him by staying away, but my spirit was being wounded more and more each day. I lost my compass, I no longer knew what my life meant, and I developed a fatalistic view of the world. You see, if not even God can protect you, there is no safe haven. If what will happen, will happen, we as individuals have no control. We are drifting aimlessly in the stream, washing up against one shore and then slamming into another. We do not have even the ability to change our direction unless God chooses to reach out His hand and help us. If He chooses not to, we drown, and I was angry, so angry, that He had chosen not to reach out His hand to help us.

I suppose the answers would have come much sooner had I prayed. I tried, but I had no idea what to say. I did not want to praise Him, I did not want to ask Him for anything, and my sense of thanksgiving was definitely skewed. Still I wanted so much to sense Him again; I was so lonely without Him and so afraid to be with Him.

During this time I had a dream. In my prior dreams I had envisioned Jesus in a beautiful white robe, sitting on a rock underneath a willowy tree. This dream was the same; He was sitting there reading a book to the children sitting on the ground before Him. I had seen this picture so many times in my mind. I would often lay my head on His lap, and He would reach his hand down and stroke my hair as I told Him of my love. I wanted to do that again. I wanted to walk over there, to put it all down and fall at His feet and just be with Him again.

As I started toward Him I noticed that between He and I was an immense brick wall that had never been there before. It was too high to climb, too long to go around and too solid to break down. I spent most of the night devising a plan to get back to Jesus. Everyone looked so happy over there, and I wanted to be there too; but I was tired and could not do it. I tried repeatedly to climb the wall or to knock it down. Finally, in exhaustion, I cried out to Jesus. "I don't know how to get over there! I don't know how to take the wall down."

He looked over at me with such love and compassion and simply said, "One brick at a time."

When I awoke I knew there would be no easy answer. I had to make a conscious decision to take the wall down. It was up to me. I had to remove the bricks if I wanted that life with Him again. Knowing that in my head did not mean knowing it in my heart. But it was enough to make me pray again. The first prayers were awkward and difficult, but at least He and I were talking. I was encouraged by reading the scripture that this was in fact a predictable end to such a journey. My family had never been promised refuge in the Lord if we did His will; we, like everyone else, were subject to another's free will. Colton, Marissa, Cain, Shin, Johnny— all of us had free will. This was what created the unpredictability of life. It was not about our relationship with each other, instead only about our relationship with God. I came across a poem written by Mother Teresa that I could not have understood prior to this; now I did.

The Call to a Holy Life

People are often unreasonable, illogical and self-centered;
Forgive them anyway.

If you are kind,
people may accuse you of selfish, ulterior motives;
Be kind anyway.

If you are successful, you will win some false friends and
some true enemies;
Succeed anyway.

If you are honest and frank, people may cheat you;
Be honest and frank anyway.

What you spend years building,
someone could destroy overnight;
Build anyway.

If you find serenity and happiness, they may be jealous;
Be happy anyway.

The good you do today, people will often forget tomorrow;
Do good anyway.

Give the world the best you have, and it may never be
enough;
Give the world the best you've got anyway.

You see, in the final analysis it is between you and God;
It was never between you and them anyway.

Mother Teresa

I had developed a tendency to look at my own pain and not at the pain of others. The pain of Mother Teresa was great, and yet her faith was so much greater. I was not proud of how I had been caught up in my own grief, but the truth is that I felt so much of it. I grieved the loss of my children, but I also grieved the loss of my purpose. I felt that for so many years we had given these children the opportunity to succeed. We had worked so hard for so long, and yet in the end we had made no difference. I often wondered what would have happened if we had not chosen to adopt these children and how their lives would have turned out. In my sadness I often believed that all of it, all ten of those years, had been for naught.

I struggled with that in my relationship with God. I had prayed the same prayer since I was a child—that He would use me, that He would find purpose for my life—and yet through the pain, heartbreak and shame I saw none. I still had not accomplished anything on His behalf. In my brokenness, I continued to pray. God spoke to me yet again in another dream. This time I was walking with Him on his journey to Golgotha. I was weeping because I did not want Him to bear the pain. He looked at me and said, "I never wanted you to bear that pain, but it was yours to bear as this is Mine." When we arrived at the terrible place where I knew He would be crucified, He said to me, "Simon from Cyrene helped me carry this cross. His gift was no less valuable because our journey still ended at this place or because he couldn't change what was about to happen. His gift was his gift, and it bore its own purpose. Your gift is only your gift, and even though the outcome is no different, the journey was."

When I awoke I felt for the first time the sadness that Christ felt for our journey, and I knew He had been there all along. But I had refused to look toward Him; it was so much easier to look away. How could I have been angry with Him for allowing each of us the gift of free will? My family had helped carry a cross for ten years, and yet maybe we ended at the same place, as if we had not helped. But our gift was our gift, and it bore its own purpose. God had not allowed this to happen to us. It simply happened to us, and He stood with us the whole time. I had chosen to walk alone, but He was there for this journey.

With that understanding I could no longer be angry and indifferent. I should have predicted such an end. I looked at Jesus' words in John 15:18-20: "If the world hates you, keep in mind that it hated me first. If you belonged to the world, it would love you as its own. As it is, you do not belong to the world. That is why the world hates you." He went on to say in 16:4, "I have told you this, so that when the time comes you will remember that I warned you." I had not remembered, and then I had blamed God for my not remembering.

My fatalistic attitude was beginning to dissolve amidst this wisdom. I could not control other people, which was a shame, but I could control how I reacted to them and allowed them to affect me. More important, I could no longer allow any of that to affect my relationship with God. I understood that; I also understood the hard part was yet to come.

It had been a year and a half since Colton and Marissa had left, and we had still not gone back to church. We had been a few times. Luckily we were in Mexico at Christmas and went to midnight mass there—no commitment, no relationships; we went because it was easy. We had also visited several different churches, but we always managed to find something wrong with each of them. In a way it was probably for the best that we had not made a commitment prior to this because we had nothing of real value to bring to a church; we were too wrapped up in our own pain.

My friend Monet kept encouraging me to go to church with her. She had walked away from our previous church the day we did. We never talked about it; she was just that kind of friend. She would not leave me alone about going back to church, though; she was also just that kind of friend. I could not find any motivation. I knew it was going to take something big because I wasn't the only one who did not want to go; no one in the family did. In fact, Amy was vehemently opposed.

Suddenly it was Ash Wednesday. It was time to find the basic childhood comforts of my faith, which included making a Lenten sacrifice. I thought of all the things I could do for Lent—give up chocolate, read the Bible more, do chores for other people—but the one thing that kept coming back to me was that we needed to go to church. I personally made the commitment that for the six weeks of Lent we would attend church every weekend regardless of what we thought of the church; we would just go.

Needless to say, there was much opposition, but no one could deny me my Lenten obligation so we all went—Joe, me and all the kids. The first few weeks I cried through the entire service. Amy cried with me, and I saw the boys on their knees praying with the same passion they had before this happened. I even saw Joe's eyes tear up as he felt the presence of God in our lives again. Toward the end of Lent I felt terrible for making this my sacrifice. I loved this church and looked forward to attending every week. It felt so good to be home. It was no sacrifice; it was a gift.

In many ways this church is a better fit for us. It was and is very community oriented. It is an outreach, always requiring its members to give back what has so freely been given to them. We were only there four months when we went on our first mission trip. We started building relation-ships with other members and close friendships, although very tentatively at first; we at least began the long process of healing. We were accepted, and we found our home.

In retrospect we do bear some responsibility for what happened with our former church. God had whispered to both Joe and me on several occasions that we were not where He wanted us. We were not blind to the obvious deficiencies within the church in respect to how it ministered not only to its members but also to those outside the church. Still we ignored the whispers. The children were so happy there; they wanted so much to stay. We did not want to take it away from them. It was difficult to accept that as parents we had failed them. We had given them what they wanted and not what they needed.

In finding forgiveness for the church, the pastor, the youth pastor and several others who had abandoned us, I had to accept that I bore some responsibility in that also. I chose to walk alone. It is true they never reached out to us, but I never reached back to them. I have never been good at asking for help, and it was a church that seemed to respond only to people's requests; I had no request.

I have no longer any anger toward the church or its leaders. We had given freely of our talents and of ourselves, and I suppose we expected them to give back to us, in at least the virtues of trust, respect and truth. That was our failure; we can have no expectation, not even of those things. When one gives, the gift is all there is.

Looking toward God again was not nearly as difficult as I had once imagined. He required so much—for us to forgive all those involved, to humble ourselves in church again, and to reach out in trust and faith—but He did not require us to do this alone. He walked with us as He always had.

I was reminded of a poem by Oliver Wendell Homes:

Always Sail, Never Drift

*"I find the great thing in this world is not so much where
we stand,
as in what direction we are moving:
To reach the port of heaven, we must sail
sometimes with the wind and sometimes against it,
but we must sail,
and not drift, nor lie at anchor."*

We had drifted for years not able to envision where we were going or how to get there, and now we had spent the last two years lying at anchor, afraid to take it up. Nevertheless, despite the fear, it was again time to sail…

Chapter Seventeen

Understanding and Acceptance

The sun was now beginning to set on this very long day. I looked around me at the porch, this morning desolate and deserted, now blossoming again with the anticipation of new growth. It was a long winter, but now it was spring; my heart sensed it. Like the flowers I had lain dormant for such a long time, but now I too had been pruned, and what was left was even more beautiful than before the storm.

I finally accepted that I, like this beautiful rosebud, had not died. This rose had sprouted from a neglected and withering vine, a vine that had suffered the harshness of the seasons, the brutal heat of the sun and the frigid cold of the winter, yet had found the strength to survive. It had found its own perfection, not dependent on anything other than its own inner strength.

The vines that had been strangling me—my cynicism, lack of forgiveness and desperate need to stay in my own place of pain—had been cut away. The dead leaves of resentment and bitterness had been cleared, and I was left with the new growth of possibility.

Nevertheless, winter does not become summer without a season of transition. I had found that season. As with spring there would be warm days where I could feel the sun's embrace, but there would also be stormy days to remind me how unpredictable each moment and each life are. It is exactly that element of unpredictability that offers us, not fear of the harshness of the past, but instead, hope of the gentleness of the future.

About this time we received a rather ominous letter. The return address was from a therapist; the handwriting was undeniably Colton's. Joe and I each took our turn staring at the envelope trying to gather the courage to open it. I am not sure why we were so afraid. The truth is, when it came to Colton, we knew no other emotion than fear.

I have always been overly optimistic, so I held the envelope in my hand and hoped for all the things any mother would. I knew there was more than an equal chance it was hateful and vile, but I hoped for the love I still deceived myself into believing was there. My hands were actually shaking when I carefully opened the flap of the envelope and began slowly to read each word.

The letter started with some small talk about what he was doing, where he was going to school, and about his job. I was touched by one particular line. He wrote, "I know we are as far apart as the left side of the rainbow is from the right." That was so important to me because I instantly thought back to the day of the adoption and the giant rainbow on his cake. I had always remembered that, but for the first time in two years I realized he did as well. I so often wondered if he believed the lies he was telling, if he had convinced himself they were true. This simple line made me think it was possible he remembered the way things really were.

The letter went on to say, "I am sorry for all the pain that I have caused the Hannah family. I thank you for reading this letter and would like to invite you to a therapy session with me. Sincerely, Colton Hannah (Biff)." How funny he would sign it Biff, since that was the nickname we called him. He did remember; I was sure of it now. This sentimental moment was interrupted by the stark reality of seeing him again. Could we as a family endure more? We had somehow made it through all this. How could he ask us to endure more? How could God?

I had read the letter aloud and forgot that Joe, too, was trying to process what he was hearing. I finally found the courage to look over at him, and his face said it all. There were no words for what he was going through. Only a parent who has lost a child and, though hopeful for his return, is fearful of it could ever understand. We did not speak. We put the letter down. With tears streaming down my face I thanked God that the last word I ever heard from my son was not what he had said to me as he walked out the door that night or in those terrible phone calls. His last word was one of kindness.

I was afraid to show the kids the letter. I had asked so much of them over the years. Did I really want to ask this of them? Did I want them to put their hearts out there yet again, not knowing what would happen? Still this was their brother; they had lived with him for ten years and would have to make this decision on their own. Therefore I let each one read it alone and then have some time to process it before we discussed it. Joey and Paul were excited and happy; they missed Colton. Amy was apprehensive. She said she would need to work through some things before she could consider this. Amanda was absolutely against the idea, and Willy said he did not want to consider it until he was at least eighteen. We told them they could each make their own decision.

The telephone number of the therapist was included in the letter. I was to call her and schedule the session if we were so inclined. I thought it would be best to talk to her one on one before we made that decision. We would take her advice as to where she thought Colton was and if he was truly ready for this.

I called the therapist and was so relieved when the answering machine came on. "You have reached Tammy White. Please leave a message." This was perfect. I could leave a message. She would think we actually had the strength to meet with Colton, and yet I would not have to schedule the meeting. Then, and in the future, I would check caller ID before I answered the phone and make sure she could not get hold of us. We were leaving for vacation in only a couple of weeks; I wanted to buy some time.

Later that afternoon the phone rang, and the caller ID said Weiss. Not recognizing the name I picked up the phone. To my surprise it was the therapist. "Hello, this is Tammy Weiss," she said. I had messed up; she did not say White on the answering machine as I had thought; instead she had said Weiss, and now with no preparation I was on the phone with her.

She informed me she had been working with Colton since he pled guilty. She had seen him for several months, and he was making real progress. She said that although he had not passed his initial lie detector test he had passed the most recent one. She said he had always been sure the bridge between our families had been irrevocably broken and with the restraining order in place had not tried to contact us; but he did want to see us. Finally she said how happy she was that we were not resistant to that possibility.

I realized I had not said anything. I had listened, but no words came to me. She had finished speaking, and all I could do was pause in the awkward silence. After what seemed like several minutes, although I am sure it was only seconds, I said, "Well, we do want to see him, but unfortunately we are going out of town and will be gone for three weeks so it will have to be after we get back. Besides, I would like to write him a letter before we see each other so he knows where we are coming from."

"Fine," she said. "That's a good idea for you to write a letter, but I hope you can get that done and still have a chance to meet with him before you leave. He would like to meet with you and Joe first and then with the siblings—any of whom would like to see him."

"OK," I said cautiously, knowing I did not intend to write this letter quickly. The longer it took, the more time we would have before we had to see him. I had mixed feelings. I wanted to see him, but I did not know if I could handle it emotionally. I knew he could say nothing to make this right; yet I wanted to hear every word he had to say.

That night, contrary to what I had told myself, I sat down to write the letter. I wanted to write about how much he had hurt us and ask him how he could do such things to a family who loved and adored him. I wanted him to know what happened to us after he left. I wanted him to feel our pain, but those were not the words that came. Instead I wrote, "In ten years we were not able to show you what unconditional love is. Maybe in one moment we can, by saying we forgive you." I went on to write that he would never know our pain and maybe that was good because we would never want anyone we loved to know that kind of pain. I acknowledged the difficult times he must have had after he left our home, the shelter, the foster home, jail. I let him know we knew he too suffered.

I wrote the letter, but each of us signed it. Everyone concurred; Colton was forgiven. Well, that is, everyone except Amy and Willy. Willy did in fact sign the letter, but he had serious reservations. The rest of us fell back, at least for a short time, into that place of hope. We were hopeful, not that Colton would again become that child we once knew, because maybe that child never existed, but instead that he could become the person we knew he had the promise to be.

I understood I had believed too much before and not questioned enough. I acknowledged I had been easily deceived and he and Marissa probably had their share of laughs about my gullibility. Nevertheless I chose to believe yet one more time that there was hope. I had wanted to take forever to write this letter and mail it to be sure we were out of town by the time he received it. Instead I put it in the mail to the therapist the following morning. Little did I know Colton had therapy the following day and would get the letter then.

The next afternoon the therapist called. She said Colton had read the letter so intently, clutching it as if someone would try to take it from him. She said he read it and then read it again and was almost giddy with excitement. All she wanted to know was when we could meet him. We scheduled it for the following Wednesday, the day before we were to leave on our trip. That seemed appropriate. If it went badly, at least we were leaving town directly after; if it went well, how much sweeter would the vacation be. It was easy to set the appointment—at least easier than it was to anticipate the meeting for the whole next week.

Each day anxiety grew; feelings of excitement and wishful thoughts were mixed with feelings of dread and impending doom. There was no peace, only constant confusion. Further, how could I tell anyone we had decided to walk back into this? I kept thinking of that old quote: "Deceive me once, shame on you; deceive me twice, shame on me." The problem was they had already deceived us twice; we were on the third time, and the shame was on everybody. I thought anybody who knew of the situation and believed the truth about what had happened would think we were foolish to take this next step. Still we had to take it.

I felt physically ill the morning of our meeting. I had concocted so many different scenarios in my mind of what could happen that I was nauseous. I tried to busy myself with packing and pretending this meeting was never going to happen, but my racing heart and sweaty palms served to remind me it was. Joe came home from work early. He had originally planned to take the entire day off, but I am sure he too needed the distraction. He asked me if I wanted to go to lunch with him before we went to the therapist's office. I shook my head no. I just wanted to go; the sooner we went, the sooner it would be over.

I remember thinking, as we were walking to the car, how much it felt as if we were going to a funeral. This made no sense because in a way Colton had been dead, and now he was alive again to us. It made no sense, but still I felt it. I knew it would take only about fifteen minutes to get there, and we were leaving too soon. But I did not want Colton to worry, not even for a moment, that we were not going to show up. We actually arrived about twenty minutes early. The therapist called us into her office, and we sat waiting and watching the door for our long lost son.

The phone rang, and I overheard Tammy say, "Colton." I could not believe it; after all this, he was the one who was not going to show. I felt my eyes well up with tears, and I bit my lip, silently berating myself for falling into this yet again.

She hung up the phone and laughingly informed us that Colton was so nervous he had spilt his coffee down the front of his shirt, and he and his foster mom were stopping to get him a new shirt because he wanted to look nice for this meeting.

I didn't think I could take this another minute. The emotions were up and down; one minute I hated him, and the next I loved him so much. I prayed the time would pass because I knew that once I saw him, once I looked into his eyes, I would know the truth. I would know if he was truly sorry. Then I snickered to myself, "How would I possibly know that? I had been wrong about everything else. Why would I know that?"

Suddenly the door opened, and in walked Colton. No knock, no time to prepare—he was just there and was running toward me. I stood, and he grabbed me and held me tighter than I had ever been held in my life.

He said, "My knees are shaking. I think I'm going to fall down." I held him tighter. We both cried—no, we both wept. We wept with sadness and with joy. We wept for the time lost and the time we now had. We could not let go of each other. I sensed Joe standing behind me, waiting his turn, but I could not let go of my son. He was part of me, and I wanted him back.

Finally Joe reached in to get his hug. It was not the same as mine. It was a sideways, one-armed hug. Joe had been able to do what I had not. He had held his emotion until he could find out more. I had simply fallen back into my role of mother, and I was again vulnerable and open. He would protect himself, for at least a moment. I envied that.

Tammy intervened. "Let's sit down." I sat back down next to Joe on the couch, and Colton sat on the other couch. "Well, how do you feel?" Tammy asked.

"May I sit over next to him?" I asked. "I just need to touch him."

"Sure, go ahead," she said.

With that, I popped up and joined Colton. He put his arms around me, and I snuggled in. We held each other's hands and never let go for the entire hour. I found at times we were just staring into each other's eyes. He was so handsome, and his eyes looked so clear; they looked so honest. He was talking, but the words were echoing; they were not of importance, at least not to me. I am sure Joe was listening intently, and I could question him later. For me, I would just bask in the love I had for my son.

There were no hard questions. All the things I had thought I would ask him, I did not. There was no answer that could make it right. I had to choose to forgive him exactly where he was, with no explanation or excuses. It was what it was, and I was certain I could live with that as long as I had him.

He told us about his time in the first foster home and that when he returned to jail the second time he decided to come clean. I told him that, despite all the horrible things he had done to us, the greatest gift he gave us was not making us endure a trial. It was his decision to tell the truth and testify against Marissa that prompted her confession. I told him I would forever be grateful for that.

Then he said something that caught my attention. "I have tried to figure out why I did what I did. I had the 'Brady Bunch' family and threw it all away. It started so simple. I wanted Desiree to feel sorry for me so I made up the story. But then it kept getting bigger, and she told someone, and they told someone. Pretty soon it was so big that I couldn't take it back."

He went on to say, "The best I can figure out is when I was taken from my biological family I had no say in that. I was not able to decide I did not want that life; it was taken from me. I did not make the decision to be a foster child, to be adopted or to live the kind of life you gave me. I wanted the chance to make that decision for myself. When I left I was sure I wanted none of what had been decided for me. One day, though, I woke up at the foster home on the east side. There was no money; there were crack dealers outside my door. No one cared, not even a little, about me. I was allowed to do whatever I wanted as long as I hooked up the foster parents with a little something. I went to a school that was run over by gangs and violence. I myself got involved with drinking and drugs; I was living my biological mother's life. That morning I finally made the decision. I did not want that life; I wanted the life you showed me. I guess I just needed to make that decision myself."

"I can understand that," I interjected. "I can understand everything, running away to be with your girlfriend, wanting to make your own decisions, all of it. The only thing I cannot understand is why you would come against us like that. Why didn't you just leave? Why did you leave and then try to destroy everything you left behind?"

"I didn't know you were still trying to help us. I didn't know you had paid Roseanne Dempster so we wouldn't have to go into Social Service custody. I didn't know about anything. I just figured after everything we did you would never want us back anyway. I also figured if I said those things about you guys, it would at least take all the attention off what we did." He looked in my eyes as he told me all this. I had to remind myself, more than once, of everything that had happened because I realized I was already trying to forget it.

Before we knew it the hour was over. I had definitely monopolized his time. I felt that I had not given Joe a chance to have any of his questions answered; he merely watched. To hurry us along, Tammy stood. Colton and I stood, but we never let go of each other. He had his arm around me, and mine was around him.

"Colton, who do you want to meet with next?" Tammy asked.

"Whoever will see me," Colton answered with a smile.

"OK. How about when you get back you bring in everyone who wants to meet with him and we have a family session?" Tammy asked in closing.

We were walking toward the door as we were talking; suddenly I looked up, and we were there. It was the moment I needed to let go of him. He needed to go back to his foster home, and we needed to go to our home, one that had not included him for a long time. I stopped briefly by his foster mother and told her how much I appreciated everything she was doing. Then I told Colton how much I loved him. He told me he loved me. I kissed him on the cheek, we had one last hug, and then it was over.

I thought I would be so happy when this was finally over. I was not; I knew we had so much hard work ahead of us if we were going to be a family again, but I wanted to bring him home right then. I wanted my family back. This melancholy soon gave place to an exuberating feeling. I had my son back.

"Let's go to lunch," I said to Joe.

"I thought you weren't hungry."

"That was before. I am definitely hungry now," I answered. It was four o'clock, and we had not eaten all day.

We went out to a late lunch, and I don't think I stopped talking the entire time. Now I was giddy; Joe just smiled. I know he found pleasure in my excitement and joy. He wanted it for me, even if he did not allow it for himself. I was happy he didn't try to take it away from me. He could have easily said, "Deb, what are you doing? You know we can't trust him." He never said that or anything else to spoil my joy. He just listened, smiled and allowed me to experience my genuine happiness.

I promised myself I would downplay it when we got home. After all, if I was making a mistake I did not want the kids to make the same one. I wanted them to take it slow, be objective, look for the truth—all the things I had not done. I did not keep this promise. I walked in the door, and with the same enthusiasm I had with Joe I told the kids about our meeting.

I'm not sure what they believed. I didn't trust myself to interpret their feelings. I wanted to protect them, but at the same time I wanted to teach them about the true gift of forgiveness. I felt lighter for I had taken the burden of sadness and loss and removed it from my back. I wanted this for them as well. We had a wonderful night preparing for our trip. We reminisced about some happy times, memories we had not allowed ourselves to think of because they had invoked such sadness. We shared these stories with each other while we packed, and we shared them with laughter.

We had a fantastic vacation. The thought of Colton returning to us only added to my joy, and I sensed it in the kids as well. Joe was still guarded, but I also sensed in him a tiny bit of hope. We each felt joy; it was undeniable.

We returned a few weeks later on a Monday afternoon, and our family therapy with Colton was on Wednesday. I wondered if the kids would feel the same apprehension Joe and I had before our meeting. I don't think Joey and Paul did. Amanda was back at school so I did not have a chance to check in with her, but Amy and Will were struggling. The plan was that we would have therapy for an hour or so, and then we would be able to take Colton to lunch and visit if we wanted to.

This time Colton was already there when we arrived. He stood up and hugged Joe and me. Reluctantly Joey and Paul went over to him and shook his hand. Amanda and Amy said hello to him and Will held back behind the rest of us so he did not have to acknowledge Colton. We all sat down, and Colton pulled up a chair in front of us. It was as if he were on the hot seat about to be grilled. There was an uncomfortable silence; Colton mostly looked down and shook his head. "I can't believe this," he kept repeating.

Joey talked first. "Did you break into my car?"

"Yes, I did. I stole your paintball gear, but it was my friend who stole your stereo," Colton answered.

"Why? Why did you make it so personal? What did I do to you?" Joey asked.

"Nothing. It wasn't about that. I just wanted my stuff, and I saw yours there and took it too."

Joey just shook his head.

Amy then said, "I have a question. The night you and I sat on the stairs for about two hours and discussed your relationship with Desiree—was any of that real?"

"No, well, maybe I meant it right then, but it wasn't real."

The tears streamed down Amy's face. Then Paul spoke. "Do you remember what you and I did the night before you ran away?"

"Yes, we dressed up in our Halloween 'scream' costumes and ran around the pond in the dark," Colton answered.

"Did you know then that you were going to run away that night?" Paul asked.

"No, I mean I knew I was going to leave. I just didn't know when."

Now Paul just shook his head. Neither Amanda nor Will spoke. When Tammy finally pushed Amanda about her true feelings, she was not able to access them. Will sat with his arms crossed in front of his chest, his head turned downward, and refused to engage.

Tammy then looked over at us and said, "How did your family survive this? Most families would have fallen apart under the stress." That was the first time anyone had acknowledged our strength. Colton had admitted the truth, and now we were not being accused; we were being acknowledged. Somehow Colton's word had become so much more valuable than ours.

"Through the grace of God" could be our only response.

Colton then asked if we wanted him to contact our former church and our friends to tell them the truth. It was so odd; I had once thought this was so important. I had once cared so much what others thought of us. Yet I did not even want him to bother; their faith or trust in us now meant nothing. I realized then how freeing it had become to lose our reputation. For the first time in my life I truly did not care what others thought of us. I had discovered who I was and who we were, and the opinion of someone else had no impact on that.

"No, Colton, we just need to work through this right now," I responded.

Tammy said then, "Well, with that in mind we cannot go forward without complete honesty, not just in what has happened but what is happening now. So with that, Colton has something to tell you."

Colton took a deep breath and began. "Saturday night my friend and I wanted to see each other for my birthday. I met him at the old foster home, he helped me stay out of trouble, and he's a good kid. I snuck out of the window of my foster home, and I used their car so we could go out."

"No, Colton, you stole their car. You did not use it," Tammy interrupted.

"I stole the car, but I did not have any intention of keeping it. We were just going to go out for a little while, and then I was going to sneak back in. We went to the park, and we accidentally fell asleep. When I got back to the foster home, my foster parents had locked the window I used to get out and I had no way to get back in, so they found out I took the car."

"Colton, you don't even have a license, and you took their car," Joe asked.

Colton nodded his head.

My heart sank. I knew one thing for sure. If two boys snuck out a window and stole a car in an effort to celebrate a birthday, the adrenaline would have been way too high for them then to have gone to a park and accidentally fallen asleep. I knew this was not the truth. One look around the room told me I was the last to get it.

At that point I sensed a real change in the room. The children had started to communicate, but now they had nothing to say; Joe did. "Colton, I want to be really clear with you. I do not believe for a moment that you fell asleep in the park. I have heard all that before. Listen. You told me you wanted to work things out and get your life back together, and then you snuck out and stole a car. I will make you a promise right here and now. I am through if there is one more incident like this. The rest of the family can continue if they want to, but I won't be back."

Colton made no response. I looked over to see Joe looking at each child individually. By this time both Amy and Amanda were crying. Joey and Paul were visibly upset, but I didn't think it was about the car as much as it was about the lie. They just could not risk it again.

Suddenly Joe, in a very protective move, pointed to the kids and said, "I will not let you hurt them again; you have done enough." Colton nodded; I sensed he knew the serious-ness of what Joe had just said.

That was it; the hour was over. We had made some prog-ress in that dialogue had been reestablished, but we had also lost ground in that we all knew Colton had not been honest with us. Tammy thought it would be a good idea if each of us met individually with Colton to communicate our feelings, our expectations and our level of commitment. To my surprise Colton agreed, and to my further surprise Joey volunteered to go first. Therapy between them was set for the following Wednesday.

Tammy then informed us there was a slight hitch in our plan to go to lunch. Part of the probation requirements Colton was subject to stated he could not be with anyone who had not attended a class on the supervision of sexual perpetra-tors. We could attend a class the following month, but as for now we would need a supervisor.

We were pleased when the foster mother, who had already completed the class, volunteered to go with us. We had a nice lunch, guarded but pleasant. The foster mom, an older woman, obviously loved Colton. She spoke of what a great kid he was and how he helped out so much around the house; she was truly taken with him. The other children opened up a little, and even a few funny memories were discussed. We talked with Colton about going out together as a family, and he said he would like to go bowling so we planned it for the following week after therapy.

The morning of our meeting Tammy called and said she thought we should take it a little slower. She said she had spoken with Colton, and he was very angry to learn she was not going to approve the bowling. She was only going to approve individual counseling sessions between each of us and Colton until some of the issues were resolved.

It was Joey's turn. I knew this would be difficult for him because he and Colton had been so close. I also knew Joey had a lot of anger and unresolved feelings for Colton. I don't know exactly how the session went, but when Joey came home he said he felt better. He said he had been able to tell Colton everything he felt and it seemed as if Colton heard him. Joey said the session was extremely difficult for Colton because Tammy was there to make sure he didn't take the easy way out of any of the questions; instead he had to think about them and give the most honest answer he had.

Mandy went to see him the following week, and then Amy the next. I tried not to get too personal about what went on at the sessions, but I listened if they wanted to talk. I gathered from all three of them that Colton listened to what they had to say about how much this had hurt them and seemed genuinely remorseful. Each of them, though, asked him the same question of why, to which he had no response. He said he did not know why he turned against the family the way he had and that was what he was concentrating on in therapy—why?

The next week was my turn, and even though I had seen him twice now, I was still nervous. I bought a little gift to take to him and even planned some of the things I wanted to say. I wanted so much to see him; yet my stomach was in knots that morning wondering how it would go. I was ready, showered and dressed several hours before I had to leave.

I was just sitting there, contemplating what was about to happen and being a little nostalgic on where we had been.

Just then the phone rang. I saw it was Tammy, and I answered joyfully because I thought she must be calling to say we were moving the meeting up since Colton was already there. Unfortunately that was not what she had to say. She informed me Colton had run away again. He had left in the middle of the night, and no one had heard from him. She said that even if he came back there would be no more therapy because she was going to recommend his probation be revoked and he be returned to jail. In one minute the dreams I had of our family being reunited and overcoming the past two years were shattered. I was left sitting there all alone; a tear started down my face, and I angrily wiped it away. I knew I could not cry again. I had shed so many tears over something that was never going to be, and I knew I needed to let it go.

I was angry with Tammy because I had asked her if Colton was ready for this. I did not want to bring my family back into this only to have them hurt again. She assured me he was authentic in his desires to be with us again. She was a therapist; she should have seen the deceit in him. Then I realized the thing that upsets us most about other people is usually the same thing we see in ourselves. I was angry because she did not see through Colton, as I had not seen through him.

I was saddened for the foster mother; I knew her pain. In some ways I thought it might even be deeper than ours because the "first cut is always the deepest." Colton had only stayed with her for a little over a year, but time is of little importance when you open your heart. We understood what it felt like to wake up and find him gone, and I wished I could take that from her.

We have not heard from Colton again. We later learned he had contacted his biological aunt, the same one Marissa had, and she paid for him and his friend to stay on the run. He was picked up later by the police, served only a short time in jail and then was released into her custody and, as far as we know, still lives with her on a farm about sixty miles from here.

He never completed the sexual offenders' program or any of the other requirements of his probation. Since he was a juvenile and served those few weeks in jail, he was released on time-served. In the end running was the best thing he could have done for himself. He was able to dissolve two years' worth of responsibilities in less than a month.

Even though it turned out the way it did, it helped us to have those few meetings with Colton to understand what had happened to us. He did not know all the answers for the things he had done, but he remembered the life he had and the love we had for him. I began to understand that perhaps Colton's life had not turned out differently because we had taken him in. But maybe the lives of his children would be; he remembered what a family was, and even though it scared him on some level he knew.

In the year to come Colton would reach out again, this time to our extended family and friends; this would cause even more division. He could not find the strength to reach out to us again, but he could not sever that bond either. We all knew Colton would never be out of our lives entirely; he would work his way back in. Our job was going to be to let him in and not allow ourselves to be taken in.

We never heard from Marissa again; we accepted that we would not. We learned through the court system that she was in fact pregnant with Max's baby and they were still living together. We also heard that since she still had not passed a lie detector test and had not truly committed to therapy Social Services would very possibly intervene and take the baby when it was born. She was a sex offender, and without treatment there was concern for the baby. This was probably the hardest news of all. Not only had we not made a considerable difference in her life, but we had also perhaps not affected the next generation. Months later we learned she had told all to her therapist and passed the lie detector test. However, she continued to deny the allegations publicly and maintained she was the victim. She and Max eventually separated; Marissa claimed he was abusing her. Marissa and baby moved in with Colton in the trailer on the biological aunt's property and remain there. The court is currently seeking revocation of Marissa's probation.

Losing two children you have raised for over ten years as your own is, I believe, one of the most difficult things a person can go through. The acceptance of this loss was so much more difficult than if they had actually died. If they had died, we would have known they did not want to leave us, and family and friends would have supported us. And even though we would have mourned and grieved for them we would have had our memories to comfort us and sustain us. As it was, they chose to leave us; they betrayed us not just by choosing to leave but by the many allegations they made when they left, the same allegations that tainted the minds of our family and friends with doubt. Still, of everything we lost, the memories were the hardest.

I had found understanding through our meetings with Colton, and I had even found acceptance through the silence of Marissa. What I had not found was how to go on from acceptance to visualizing our new reality without them.

Chapter Eighteen

The Conclusion

I was finally finished with this long day of work. The porch, although not exactly as it had been before, was restored. It was not closed off anymore; it was open and inviting. There were scars from the neglect and abuse, but only we could see those scars now. To a passerby, even to our family and friends, it was again beautiful.

I was troubled by that thought, because for a while there were no friends to come. Just then I began to watch the birds fly in and land on the newly filled birdhouse. They had not come for so long because there was nothing for them here. Now they sensed it was safe to come back, and I did not need to invite them; they simply came. I knew people were very much the same, and now that they could see healing in us, our lives were again beginning to become full.

I had once asked myself if this was merely the predictable end to such a journey. Years ago I could have never believed that was true, but there is truth in it. We took our journey blindly; we took an unlit path. We did not have the training, understanding and knowledge we should have. The National Foster Parent Association supports mandatory training for all foster parents. They have advised that training should take place on three separate levels—pre-service, apprenticeship and ongoing; we received none.

Their recommendations are based on the fact that over the past twenty years the kinds of children available for adoption have changed dramatically. Many of the children now available and waiting for permanent families have been abused or neglected in their early years, and many have experienced multiple placements. These children have been damaged in ways that will affect their behavior for many years.

According to the NFPA Statement on Child Abuse/Neglect Allegations in Foster/Adoptive Families, "Many children who have suffered such damage have learned maladaptive or antisocial behaviors. They are manipulative, unable to trust, lack a sense of honesty and responsibility, and are deficient in many areas of their development.

Such children, because of their histories, typically behave in ways that jeopardize the security and stability of the families diligently striving to undo some of the damage of the past and to help the children develop more appropriate and socially acceptable behaviors. These children often lie and play on the responses of other adults who do not view their behaviors in the context of the children's prior experiences. Some children deliberately hurt those who offer help and try to destroy close relationships. After a sequence of adult rejections they cannot accept that others care about or love them. It is *not* uncommon for the children themselves to make false reports of abuse/neglect in an effort to control adult behavior or to deal with fears of close relationships."

The statement further says, "Foster/adoptive parents of difficult or emotionally disturbed children are often subjected to community scrutiny and suspicion that biological families do not experience. Foster/adoptive families are sometimes highly visible in their communities due to their size or composition. Many people do not understand why someone would chose to adopt/foster older children, large numbers of children, and children with handicapping conditions or negative histories. Hence, they are suspicious of the parents' motives. This lack of understanding can also apply to agencies responsible for investigations of alleged abuse/neglect."

Finally the statement says, "Due to these factors, foster/adoptive parents can be unfairly and unduly stressed. Instead of receiving support and assistance from the community, they may be forced to expend their energies on defending themselves rather than getting on with their parenting job." The part I found most disturbing was that the NFPA made this statement in 1987, seven years before we even thought of fostering or adopting; yet never a word of these findings was ever mentioned to us.

According to the NFPA, "it is estimated that as of 1997 there was a one in eight chance of having false abuse or neglect allegations made against foster and/or adoptive parents. This number is growing and in some areas of the nation has increased by as much as 400 percent."

The possibility of allegations of abuse/neglect is real. These allegations can result from the child's understandable lack of loyalty to the new family, misunderstandings at school and with neighbors or even the community's lack of knowledge about adoption issues. It is certainly something that needs to be discussed and examined prior to taking in children. We had never done that. It had never crossed our minds, not even for a moment, that the children we loved more than life would someday come against us as if we were the enemy. Even accepting this, it is by far not the only risk a family faces.

What about reactive attachment disorder, the diagnosis of both Cain and Johnny?
The possible causes, especially during the first two years of life, include:

* Maternal drug and/or alcohol use during pregnancy
* Premature birth
* Drug-addicted infant
* Abuse (physical, emotional, sexual)
* Neglect
* Sudden separation from primary caretaker
* Frequent moves or placements

Taking into account that almost every child in the foster care system has had a separation from their primary care-taker and suffered some form of abuse or neglect, the likelihood is that each child will have some symptom of reactive attachment disorder to some level or degree. We should have anticipated this possibility and should have learned more about this disorder before we even began this process.

Cain and Johnny are the real ones who suffered because of our lack of knowledge. Often we looked to their behaviors as intentional and took much of it way too personally. Had we been equipped with the understanding of the causes, symptoms and possible treatments, we may have been better able to meet their needs. We may have been able to be better parents.

There was also the question of mental illness. We were never given medical records, diagnoses or extended family history. In fairness we were told mental illness was a factor in both Johnny and Cain being removed from their biological family, but the true focus was on the abuse they suffered at the hand of their biological father and the neglect of their mother. This became the focal point of therapy. We could have researched further into the likelihood that the disease would be passed on to the children, except that for many years we did not know what that disease was. I am sure we would still have adopted both Cain and Johnny had we known the probability that they would inherit mental illness, but how much more effective would we have been as parents had we been informed of this pertinent information.

Only recently I read that a primary factor in determining how a child will do in placement is IQ. We knew both Colton and Marissa had very low IQ scores, and we also knew Social Services was good at obtaining IQ scores on the children who came into placement. We just did not know the correlation. If a correlation does exist, it should be either Social Services or their therapist's responsibility to explain the correlation to the family.

Nevertheless, not all the blame rests on Social Services. Admittedly there are too many open cases for the number of caseworkers employed. Many of these caseworkers have a good heart for children and want to put their needs as a priority, but sometimes this is done at the expense of the families in which these children are being placed. Important information is sometimes left out under the guise of "we just don't know."

When Johnny was taken by ambulance from day treatment to the hospital, I had a chance to speak with one of the therapists who had worked with him. She informed me it broke her heart to see the devastation some families were forced to endure after the adoption. Further, she said she had actually sat in on "round table" meetings where possible adoptive parents questioned the background and behaviors of the child they were considering. At these meetings, she said, she personally witnessed the lies and omissions made on behalf of the county agencies in order to ensure placement.

Often, she said, the needs of the child and the needs of the agency far outweighed the needs of the family. Many times the adoptive parents, the adoptive siblings and even their current living situation were not taken into account. Reality was and is that there are far more children to adopt than families to adopt them. Scaring off a family with too much information too soon was not a viable option even though this failure to transmit significant and vital information sometimes led to tragic consequences.

Ultimately we had accepted that we bore responsibility in what happened as well. We were young and naïve and believed the greatest lie of all—"that we could just love a child enough to heal him." Many of the things that happened to us could have been avoided, and even though we suffered a terrible loss, if we could go back in time, we would still have taken these children into our home. We would simply have been more aware of what we were doing. We would not have had idealized expectations; we would have had realistic hopes based on knowledge and training. Many children need a home, and many families can make a tremendous difference in their lives. Our story is not meant to discourage anyone. For every story like ours are so many stories of adoption success. Our story is told only to encourage those who have made this decision in their lives to prepare themselves to be better parents than we were and to survive better what may well be the predictable end to this journey. It is also my hope that our story will encourage and inform those who have the opportunity to support families like ours in their time of crisis. I further hope this story will persuade others to reach out, see past the allegations and innuendos, and instead search for the truth.

Adoptive and foster parents who accept troubled children into their homes and hearts need to understand the potential risks. These risks include reactive attachment disorder, oppositional defiance disorder, post-traumatic stress disorder, and possible links to mental illness, including schizophrenia and the genetic component associated with psychopathic personality. Risks further include sexual abuse and the increasing possibility of being accused of child abuse or neglect. These are only the risks we are aware of because of our experiences; there are more. To this day, however, we do not believe the risks outweigh the reward; they just need to be considered.

In the end it was true that our innocence was betrayed by the Department of Social Services in their withholding of pertinent information as well as in their not providing us with the appropriate training and long-term support we needed. It was also true that our innocence was betrayed by the people we thought would stand by us and defend us within our community. The real truth, though, is that it was not just our innocence that had been betrayed. Colton and Marissa's innocence was betrayed by the loss of their childhood and the neglect by their parents. Cain and Johnny's innocence was betrayed by the mental illness that plagued their family for generations. Will's innocence was betrayed by everyone he once counted as family. Finally, Mandy, Joey, Amy and Paul, innocent from the beginning, were betrayed by the truth.

Looking back, as I sat down and began to rock again, I accepted the role of each of us in what happened. I knew that just like these beautiful rose bushes standing before me there would always be moments in our lives when we were damaged by a storm, moments when we would lie dormant, waiting for the sun, and moments when we would bloom with the beauty only God could truly see in us.

I put down my glass of iced tea as I heard the honking of a horn and the sound of the car pulling up in the driveway. It was Joe and Mandy and Amy, Joey, Will and Paul. It was good to see the children again. Mandy is a senior at Regis University and has her own apartment near campus. She is applying to med school now as well as graduate school because she also enjoys research. Joey also has his own apartment near his campus at University of Northern Colorado. He is studying business and has formed a subsidiary of Joe's company. Amy lives in the dorm at Colorado State University; she is studying pre-law; our experiences opened her eyes to the legal system. Only Paul and Will are still at home and they graduate high school next year. They have not yet decided where they will go to college; Paul wants to play football and Will wants to wrestle, so they are considering their options. At this moment, though, they are home... a reason to celebrate.

There they were, laughing and carrying on, excited about life. They ran up on the porch as if it had always been this way. They did not seem to notice my hours and hours of labor. It was as if, in their minds, this beauty always existed; it was only I who could not see it. We sat out on the porch together, even after the sun went down, reminiscing, laughing and sharing stories.

In the end, there is a risk in every moment of life. There can be no promises or assurances, no guarantee of "happily ever after"—instead only the knowledge that, regardless of the ending, it is important to take the risk.

Henry David Thoreau once wrote, "The perception of beauty is a moral test." I understood this as I remembered the thorn that had pricked my finger earlier that morning and how I had misconstrued the betrayal of the prick, and the deep red of my blood, with the beauty of the rose. In my innocence, I had not been able to see the thorns, and in my pain, I had not been able to see the beauty that once was. It is for each of us to decide whether the beauty inherent to the rose overshadows the risk of being pierced by its thorn.

For our family, and for so many like ours, the answer has always been yes. We accepted that risk gladly, we chose that path, but we did so in the dark, and were startled by the dangers that lied before us. Nevertheless, we would have taken this path again, only this time, cautiously guided by the light of truth.

My family and I would continue to risk betrayal for beauty; we would just do our best to no longer confuse the two.

"Above all else, guard your heart,
for it is the wellspring of life."
Proverbs 4:23

My Life

*O*ne thing in my life I have learned is nothing comes easy.
*But if you put your trust in the Lord everything will be
just fine.*

*I was less fortunate when I was a child. I never had the
chance to bond with my mom and dad and grow in a true
relationship with them. At the age of four I had not had the
opportunity to learn about the love of God. So, when I was
introduced to my new family, I had no idea the plan God had
in store for me.*

*My new mom, Deb, had the biggest smile, and her hair
smelled great! Right away I felt loved, and it was in a way
that was different from how I had ever felt before. I did
not know whether to accept it or push it away. I remember
meeting my dad, Joe; he was really tall and looked stern.
After a couple of minutes of being with him, I realized he was
the nicest man there was. When I hugged him it was like I
had on an armored vest and no one could hurt me.*

*The hardest part of my new family was learning their
names; they all looked the same. The youngest, Paul, was so
small; yet he had the biggest heart and was always smiling.
Then there was Joey; I could tell after spending time with
him that he was a leader and did not have to follow anyone*

because he knew who he was. The two girls were almost identical. Amy and Amanda, they got along so well with each other and just spread their glow across the whole room.

My family is everything to me. I consider my parents my angels because without them I would not be here today. They have taught me so many things. One thing I pray every night is to become like them because then I know I have succeeded.

My brothers and sisters have taught me foremost that they will always be there for me. They have taught me never to take anything for granted, to say what is on my mind and never change who I am, if it in any way compromises my faith.

In the end God has given me the greatest, most loving and by far the most caring family. The only way I know how to thank them is to succeed. I will be the one who proves they made the right decision with their lives. I will be the reason that, despite everything that happened to them, proves they were not wrong in letting all of us come live with them. They went through a lot, and maybe my life is all they have to show for it, but they have my life.

To them I will be forever grateful.
William Hannah

The Hannah Family Prayer

*Lord, through the hard times
that You have bestowed upon us,
lift us up into Your hands,
above the fires of temptations
and through the mud of evil.
Help us to become stronger and wiser.*

*Your plan for us, Lord, is what we shall accept,
no matter the difficulty or sorrow.*

*Lord, let Your will be done.
We put our lives and our trust in only You.
We shall soon rise above and
beyond our own expectations,
as we live our lives in the grasp
of Your hands.*

*Lord, send Your angels down
on this family
to guide us through the darkness.
Reach out to those who abandoned us.
Bless them
and take them into Your heart.
We pray they accept Your love
and carry it in the depth
of their souls.*

Lord, let Your will be done.

Paul Hannah

This story is based on actual events;
some names and places have
been changed
to protect the legal rights
of those involved, as well as to
maintain confidentiality.

NOTES

Introduction: *Reflections on a Life Once Lived*
1. Bojaxhiu, Agnes Gonxha, <u>Mother Theresa Her Words</u>.
   EWTN Global Catholic Network, July 2006.
   <<u>http://www.ewtn.com/motherteresa/words.htm</u>>.

Chapter 1: *A Simple Knock*
1. Dromgoole, Will Allen. <u>Lines to Live By</u>.
   Nashville: Thomas Nelson Inc. 1972.

Chapter 5: *RAD*
1. Horn, Miriam. "A Dead Child A Troubling Defense."
   <u>U.S. News</u> July 1997.
2. Lowe, Peggy. "Rebirthing Team Convicted."
   <u>Rocky Mountain News</u>." 20 April 2001.
3. Weidman, PhD, Arthur Becker. <u>Mental Health Matters.</u>
   Get Mental Health, Inc. July 2006.
   <<u>http://www.mental-health-matters.com/disorders/dis_details.</u>
   <u>php?</u>>.
4. Gibran, Kahlil. <u>The Prophet.</u>
   Columbia University, July 2006.
   <<u>http://www.columbia.edu/~gm84/gibtable.html</u>>.

Chapter 10:   *The Kiss of Betrayal*

1. Agathon. Aristotle, <u>Nicomachean Ethics.</u>
   The Quotations Page, July 2006.
   <http://www.quotationspage.com/quote/24195.html>.

Chapter 11:   *Betrayed Again*

1. Mack, Maynard. <u>Alexander Pope: A Life.</u>
   New York, N.Y. W.W. Norton &Company, Inc. 1986.
2. Goethe, Johann Wolfgang Von.
   The Quotations Page, July 2006.
   <<u>http://www.quotationspage.com/quote/29659.html</u>>.

Chapter 14:   *Emotional Healing*

1. Kubler-Ross, Elisabeth. <u>Death and Dying The 5 stages of Grief.</u>
   About Health and Fitness. July 2006.
   <http://dying.about.com/cs/glossary/g/g_5Stages.htm>.
2. Editorial, TLC Group, <u>Article 8 - Beware the 5 Stages of "Grief".</u>
   Counseling for Loss and Life Changes, July 2006.
   <<u>http://www.counselingforloss.com/article8.htm</u>>.
4. <u>The Psychopathic Personality</u>
   Oregon Counseling.org. March, 2004
   <http://www.oregoncounseling.org/Handouts/
   PsychopathicPersonality.htm>.
5. Hare Ph.D., Robert D. <u>Without Conscience: The Disturbing World</u>
   <u>of the Psychopaths Among Us.</u>
   New York, NY: The Guilford Press, 1993.
6. Hare P.h. D., Robert D. <u>The Hare Psychopathy Checklist.</u>
   Toronto: Multi-Health Care Systems. Revised 1991.

Chapter 16:   *Spiritual Healing*

1. Shaw, George Bernard. <u>George Bernard Shaw on Humanity.</u>
   Institute for Global Ethics. Ethics Newsline, July 2006.
   <<u>http://www.globalethics.org/newsline/members/issue.</u>
   <u>tmpl?articleid=04150214475984</u>>.
2. Bojaxhiu, Agnes Gonxha, <u>Mother Theresa Her Words</u>.

EWTN Global Catholic Network, July 2006.
<http://www.ewtn.com/motherteresa/words.htm>.

Chapter 17:   *Understanding and Acceptance*
1. Holmes Sr., Oliver Wendell. Always Sail, Never Drift.
   Autocrat of the Breakfast Table. GIGA Quotes, July 2006.
   <http://www.giga-usa.com/gigaweb1/quotes2/qutopinnovationx001.htm>.

Chapter 18:   *The Conclusion*
1. National Foster Parent Association. NFPA Position Statements.
   ON CHILD ABUSE/NEGLECT ALLEGATIONS IN FOSTER/
   ADOPTIVE FAMILIES, 1987.
   <http://www.nfpainc.org/aboutNFPA/positionStmnt.
   cfm?page=1#2-4t>.
2. National Foster Parent Association. NFPA Position Statements
   ON FOSTER PARENT TRAINING, 1987.
   <http://www.nfpainc.org/aboutNFPA/positionStmnt.cfm?page=1#2-4t>.
3. Shader, Michael. Risk Factors for Delinquency: An Overview.
   U.S. Department of Justice. Office of Juvenile Justice and
   Delinquency Programs. July 2006.
   <http://www.ncjrs.gov/pdffles1/0jjdb/frd030127.pdf>.
4. Adoption things that can go wrong: Unknown/Unexpected Health
   Conditions.
   MentalHelp.net, July 2006.
   <http://mentalhelp.net/poc/view_doc.
   php?type=doc&id=10065&cn=11>.
5. Thoreau, Henry David.
   BrainyQuote. July 2006.
   <http://www.brainyquote.com/quotes/quotes/h/henryda-
   vid162027html>.

Printed in the United States
61621LVS00003BA/1-108